ABOUT THE BOOK

In a vision, Alfred the One-Legged, a young boy running from the hordes of heathen Danes invading England, was guided to an old harness and told that if he would be the master of his life, he should give the harness to his namesake. And who would his namesake be but Alfred of Wessex, later to be England's king and deliverer?

King Alfred did, indeed, have the secret to mastery over life, but to the one-legged boy it seemed a strange one. In England's bloodiest days, King Alfred taught patience and peace, learning and the written word. They were the strengths that saved England as well as young Alfred, who became the king's scribe.

"Every man," King Alfred said at Stonehenge, "is a part of the bridge between the past and the future. Whatever helps him feel this more strongly is good." Mr. Hodges has, himself, done this good thing. In this unique book he has re-created a noble hero, an exciting era, and the birth of Britain.

THE NAMESAKE

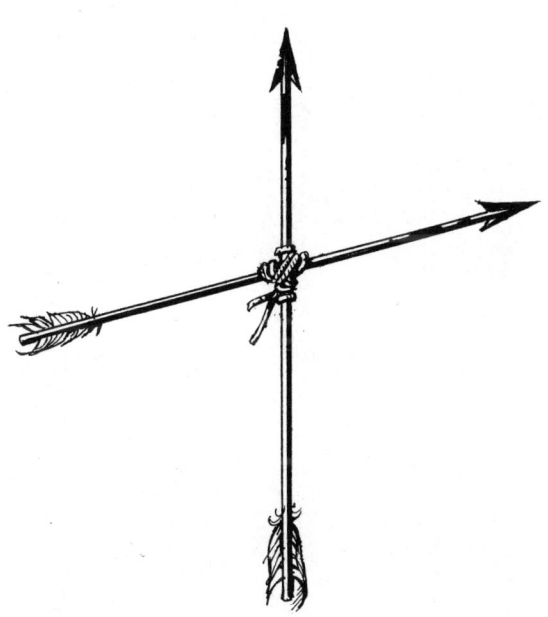

THE NAMESAKE

Written and Illustrated
by C. Walter Hodges

COWARD-McCANN, INC.   NEW YORK

Books by C. Walter Hodges

COLUMBUS SAILS

SHAKESPEARE AND THE PLAYERS

First American Edition

© 1964 by C. Walter Hodges

All rights reserved. This book, or parts thereof, may not be reproduced without permission in writing from the publishers.

Library of Congress Catalog Card Number: 64-13068

Manufactured in the United States of America

012 up

CONTENTS

		Page
1	Thornham	11
2	King Edmund	21
3	The Heathen	34
4	The Crutch and the Harness	50
5	The First Blow in Wessex	58
6	The King's Brother	65
7	King Ethelred	76
8	Three at Ashdown	89
9	The Dane-Leg	107
10	The King at Easter	119
11	A New Feeling	138
12	Departures	152
13	A View of Doomsday	164
14	Guthorm	170
15	The War in Dorset	183
16	The Dry Summer	199
17	The Ring-Oath	213
18	The Riding	227
19	Farther to Go	240
20	The Swans	250
21	A Gull Crying	256
22	Parting Words	265

1

Thornham

I, ALFRED THE ONE-LEGGED, sometimes called Alfred Timberleg or Alfred Dane-Leg, being now an old man, have returned at last to my own country of East Anglia. Here in the newly built abbey where King Edmund the Holy Martyr lies in his carved and jeweled tomb, I write this story. I write of my young days; of how as a boy I came to know and serve the King my namesake, Alfred of Wessex, England's deliverer. I tell of battles and defeats, of courage in adversity, and how in the end it was rewarded.

All this Christian land is now at peace. Englishman and Dane together plow and reap as neighbors under the same sky, and over them King Alfred's grandson rules the land in the strength and wisdom of King Alfred's law. Yet still in my mind's eye I see how thickly the smoke blew about and how the thistles grew, back there in the days of my boyhood, around the deserted farm where the dead man's legs stuck out of the ditch beside the teamless plow. I can see clearly, as though I were still that same little limping boy who watched it all long ago, how the holy King Edmund came to the church at Thornham, and how in his thin rough garment he knelt all night before the altar, praying and weeping and praying for the victory which was beyond hope, while from the darkness behind the candles the monks of Thornham intoned their Litany:

From the fury of the Northmen, O Lord deliver us!

This summer I returned to Thornham. The place is not more than eight miles from St. Edmund's Minster, yet Brother Joseph, the monk who came with me, did not even know that a monastery had once stood there, sixty years ago. There is no longer any sign of it. A large ill-kept farmstead occupies the site. I myself hesitated when I saw it, thinking the place could not be the same; yet knowing how easily we are deceived about the places of our youth, expecting them to be so much finer than we find them when we revisit them in later years, I went closer. Then as we went up the roadway from the ford I began to remember it, the slight hill and the turn at the top of it; and the shape of the little wood behind the buildings, that was much the same. But there was no sign of any familiar thing among the huts and byres at the top of the rise until we came to the farmer's dwelling hall, and here we found a door with its doorposts and lintel, and an arched wooden headpiece over it, and a wooden figure, weathered and unpainted, scarcely recognizable for a man, but which I knew to be St. Luke the Evangelist, carved within the arch. It was the old door of the writing room where the learned Brother Githo, the only one of us in that monastery who could read or write, used to keep his fowls.

I know now that it had been only a poor brotherhood at Thornham. There were not above twenty monks, with a few serfs, male and female, who had come there some years before with their master. He had been driven from his lands by the heathen, and, at his death, had bequeathed them to the monastery to pay for masses for his soul. So there the serfs remained, working with the brethren on the farm, and three urchin children who belonged to some of them were the chief friends of my youth.

Of the monastery buildings the largest were of wood, the rest of wattle and mud, and all were thatched with reeds. In the middle was the wooden church of the blessed Saint Cuthbert, to whose glory the monastery was dedicated but to which, alas, it added very little. Within the church the walls and ceilings were painted all over with a great picture of the Last Judgment, the work of one of the monks of the first settlement. This, in my time, was very old and decayed, and not for more than a hundred years had there been another monk able to repair what was peeling off, or repaint what had already gone. But what matter? All has now disappeared, painting and church, kitchen and barn, the little cells of the monks, all. A few of the old timbers had been rescued and used in the building of the present farm, into whose yard I arrived with Brother Joseph this summer's afternoon, and these, I could see, were charred in places where the destroying fire had scorched them long ago.

There was a woman in the yard as we came near. She had a child with her; but seeing me stumping along on my crutch, with my one leg, she cried out and made the sign of the cross upon herself and the child, and for better measure thrust the child away into a shed and locked the door, for fear I would put the evil eye upon it. She did the same for two young calves that were in the yard, driving them into the dwelling hall and calling loudly for the farmwife. I have long been used to such behavior, for few people have ever seen a one-legged man, and most people are ignorant and full of fears. When I was a young man and still ashamed, I used sometimes to wear a long gown to hide my loss, but its loose folds were an encumbrance against the crutch; neither could I wear it when riding a horse, as I learned to do; so I soon gave it up, and contented myself to be seen for what I am.

The farmwife came out. She glanced us over for a minute from her doorway, and then bade us come in out of the sun. She gave us milk to drink, and sent the other woman to let the child out of the shed, where it was crying loudly.

We learned that the farmer was a Dane. His name was Ketil, the farmwife told us, and his father had taken this land in the harrying, in the old days; but although the father had been baptized a Christian and had died in penitence, and although Ketil likewise was a pious man and observed every Lord's day with fasting and sacrifice, the farm was poor, the crops thin, the cattle sickly, and nothing would flourish.

"Alas," said she, "it is God's will. This land was stolen from Holy Church. So we work here not for prosperity but for punishment. Perhaps in time we will work off the curse and all will be well. Do you think so, father?"

Brother Joseph, to whom, seeing that he was a priest, she had spoken, said, "Have you asked your parish priest? What comfort does he give?"

She said, "We have no priest in this parish; but there is a holy man who lives in a cave not many miles away, and he knows the prayers for things. He has told my husband that we must put up a cross on the place where the altar of the old church used to be. Then all may be well, he says. But alas, how are we to know the place where the altar was?"

Here I understood why it was that God had sent me back to Thornham that day.

"Farmwife," said I, "I can find you the place." I told her how it was that I knew. She could hardly bring herself to believe me, in spite of her joy. And indeed I found it was no easy thing that I had promised. Until late evening I stumped and searched in the yard, in the farm buildings, often kneeling to pray for guidance to recognize some landmark, some piece of rubble. Ketil the farmer and his men came back from the fields and with their spades dug and scraped among the dunghills until at length we were able to trace a few stumps which had once been the wall posts of the church, and four patches of rubble which had been the foundations upon which stood the four roof posts. The place of the altar we found at last in the dog's kennel, where there was a great bitch like a she-wolf snarling at us over her pups. Ketil beat his forehead with his fist.

"Sacrilege, sacrilege!" he cried. "It has been the dog's place ever since my father built the farm! Small wonder we have had thin luck!" He fell to his knees and raised both hands to heaven. "See, I will kill this dog and her litter, and pour their blood on the altar place in atonement for our sin. And I will raise the cross here, as the holy man bade me, and each year on this day I will sacrifice my best dog in its shadow."

"My son, my son," cried Brother Joseph in horror. "The cross will not need the blood of these poor creatures. You need only clean the place well and I will bless it and sprinkle holy water upon it."

Ketil, although he seemed doubtful whether these measures would be strong enough to atone for such a sacrilege, was, with cooler thinking, well pleased to spare the bitch. He and his thralls did not spare their pains. At once they set about clearing away the kennel, digging, sweeping and washing out the place until, soon after sunset, with the moon rising, Brother Joseph, in the presence of all, sprinkled and blessed it as he had promised.

Brother Joseph and I were to lodge that night at the farm, and there was much coming and going, sweeping the place where we were to lie and bringing in clean straw; much clatter of pots and pans and of carrying firewood, and all the preparation of food and drink which, said the farmer, must be made worthy of such an occasion. So when all was done outside we were brought into the dwelling hall, where a single bench and table had been set for the farmer and his guests. We sat one on each side of him and were waited upon by the farmwife herself. Everyone else, men, women and children, about twenty in all, sat on the earth floor in a ring around the fire and helped themselves from several great pots that were kept warm on the hearthstone. A she-goat bleated in a corner, a pair of little pigs ran in and out, nosing for scraps, and on a beam under the low roof a line of fowls sat roosting in the smoke that rose up to find its way out through the holes in the thatch. To all this farmer Ketil, making a great gesture with his bare arm that was spotted with cow dung, and with words that might have done well for an ealdorman feasting in his high Shire hall, bade us welcome. And welcome it was, for we had not eaten since morning.

"Now," said the farmer a little later, "this is the good time of a meal, the time when one has ceased feeding one's hunger and begins to eat for pleasure. This is the time when a meal begins to be a feast. This is the time when we sing our songs, and when strangers tell us their stories. Shall we sing first, strangers, or will you tell us about yourselves?"

There was some whispering and laughing among the farm people, some pushing forward and holding back, and all eyes were on me. I knew what it was. At length, with some urging, the head man of the thralls came forward and said to Ketil, "Master, let the old man tell us about his leg."

The farmer turned to me with a grin and a shrug. "My people are brutish," he said. "But then, may my sins be forgiven me, so am I. Tell us about your leg, old man. How did it come off? Was it in battle? Was it struck off with one great sword blow, with blood spouting, with hewing and cracking, the stark shield-rending of heroes? Was it that way?"

"No," I said, "it was not that way. It was when I was a child."

"Heaven's mercy!" said they all, and crossed themselves. "A child with one leg! And yet to live so long! Yet tell us, how did it happen?"

"I do not remember," said I. "It was in the harrying and warfare of the old days when your people first came here to East Anglia. They came like wolves with the north wind, in thousands upon thousands; and not thousands of men only, but thousands of shiploads. And when they had plundered along all our coasts and up all our rivers, they left their ships and marched inland and seized all the horses in the countryside, and formed themselves into a huge army on horseback, and rode and plundered through the whole length of England."

"Three great kings they had!" cried Ketil the farmer, breaking in. "Three wicked kings together, wicked, but hoi! hoi! they were stark men and great ones! Halfdan the Black, and Ingvar, called the Boneless because he was so fat, and Hubba the yellow-bearded, who was a little man, so my father told me, quite bald and shining everywhere above his ears, but with a huge beard below, all yellow. It was said he stained it with saffron. And he was as fierce as a hungry dog. Was it he who took off your leg?"

"I remember nothing," said I again, "neither leg nor foot, nor father, nor mother, nor anything except the burning and the shouting and the folk running away. There was something that fell on me. It would have been my death, but by God's mercy there was a man hiding in the same place I had crawled into. He was a stranger from another country, I do not know where, and it was he who took off my leg for me, and so saved my life. So at least I was told afterwards. There are wise men in Spain who are said to be able to do such things. That is all I know. I was taken by some compassionate folk and left in the care of the monks here at Thornham. I grew up here with my little crutch. God is good, one gets used to these things. I helped look after the pigs and the bees, and sometimes when he thought about it, Brother Githo used to try to teach me how to read and to write. But he was old and did not think about it very often."

"To do these things, is it hard?" asked the farmer.

"To read and write? Yes, it is hard to learn," I answered. "But certain men have found it worth the trouble."

The thralls who had gathered around were all open-mouthed and blank-eyed. They did not understand.

"He means," the farmer explained to them, but carefully, as though he was himself not very sure, "he means the making of marks with black juice, as does the holy man at Hoxne."

They all crossed themselves again.

"And did you ever learn to do it?" he asked me.

"I did, but not then; for when I was ten years old, or thereabouts, the heathen armies came back again. You spoke just now of Hoxne. Do you know of the saintly King Edmund, and how the heathen slew him there?"

"Holy Edmund forgive us for our sins!" cried Ketil the Dane. "Who does not know it? And did you see him when he was alive on earth, the tall hero of God? This is your story to tell, old man. Tell us, then, how you saw him in your youth, the sad saintly king of the East English."

This I consented to do. But since they saw him in their mind's eye as he is now in Heaven, the tall hero of God, I thought it unwise to describe him as I had seen him then, a poor creature praying in the cold, so long ago.

2

King Edmund

Bareheaded and barefoot, clad in a thin shabby gown, with a gold cross on a chain around his thin neck, his thin hands clasping a golden reliquary which contained a finger bone of the blessed Saint Felix, his eyes half-closed, his lips muttering, his feet bleeding and stumbling upon the stubbled, stone-frozen fields of late November, such was Edmund, King of East Anglia, on the day that I saw him. He was still a young man, but wasted with fasting. Since the coming of the Northmen who had ravaged his kingdom up and down, he had spent his life in penitence, seeking by his own atonement to turn away this scourge of God from his people and his land.

There was a time when it seemed as though God had heard his prayers, for the heathen host had marched

away for a time into Northumbria. The three heathen kings, Halfdan, Ingvar and Hubba, were all sons of old Ragnar Hairy-Breeches, whom Aella, King of Northumbria, had thrown to his death in a pit of snakes; and so the three had a debt to pay. But when they had paid it, and slain King Aella with the ritual of the blood-eagle, and plundered his land, they came back again to East Anglia with their army, like a swarm of carrion birds returning to a familiar roost. On their way back they sacked and burned down the abbeys of Crowland and Peterborough, and many others. King Edmund wept when he heard of it. Then his thanes came to him urging him at last to give battle. "We see now that we can expect no peace from the heathen till they have picked us to the bone and cast down the Cross of Christ forever," they said. "Rise up, lord King, and send out your war banner."

The Christian army gathered at Hoxne. Their spies rode out toward Thetford and there smelled the smell of burning, and saw the crows flapping over the woods where the heathen host was encamped. They made their report. "Tomorrow we will fight," said King Edmund. "But today I will do a penance at Thornham Minster and pray for our victory." This was why he came barefooted to us over the hard fields. With him there came only his Mass priest and a few of his thanes, armed to guard him, all on foot.

At the church door our Prior, Ulfwin, met him and would have put the penance candle into his hand; but the King, putting it aside, cast himself down flat upon his face, and in this way dragged himself into the church and along to the foot of the altar. It was toward evening. It was bitterly cold in the church. The King shivered as he lay. The frosty breath of the monks chanting the Litany rose up like a moving smoke in front of the pictures of Hell and the Last Judgment painted upon the walls around. Outside the church the soldiers had lit a great fire to warm themselves.

"It is warmer fighting," said one. "And I have sometimes thought the Lord God would rather hear the din of our swords fighting to protect His Christian lands than the everlasting din of our prayers begging for the protection of His arm. They sometimes say that He helps them that help themselves."

"They sometimes say too much," said another, after a long silence. "We are the King's men. He is holy, and we have our duty."

"Tomorrow, then," said a third. "At last."

The first man said, "Better it had been two years ago."

Soon after dark, mixed with the singing of the monks in the church, there came a sound of horses. The soldiers rose to their feet. A little company of armed men rode into the firelit yard.

"Whose men are you here?" demanded their leader, reining in.

"It is the Earl Cenwulf," said one of the soldiers. "You know us, lord. We are King's thanes."

The Earl asked where the King was, and being told, he dismounted and went straightway into the church.

"We have ridden hard," explained one of the newcomers. "The heathen are marching, even now by night. By morning we shall all be slain in our tents if we don't take care. We have doubled our pickets and the whole army is standing to arms. We must have the King with us without delay. We have brought horse and armor for him. And some food," he added. "He will need a good lining to his stomach now."

After a few minutes the Earl Cenwulf came out slowly, pausing at the church door a moment as if in doubt before he rejoined the others at the fire.

"He will not—cannot come yet," he said. "He has not yet heard the Mass. The Mass will be sung"—he stood silent a moment, as though guarding something in his mind, then continued—"later. It will be later tonight. My horse!" he cried suddenly. "Stay you here, Berwyn, you and the others. If the King comes out, beg him to eat and clothe himself, and bring him as soon as you can."

He went. The men sat silent around the fire. There was silence even from the church. The Earl's distant hoofbeats died away.

A white owl swooped suddenly ghostlike out of the night, and sat upon the gable over the church door. The men crossed themselves. The owl shrieked once and flew away.

"A bad omen!" said one of the soldiers, and "Hush!" said the others, fearing to name fear. Then suddenly the one who had first spoken looked across at me. I stood not far off so that I could warm myself a little, and hear what they said.

"That boy!" cried the man. "See, he has only one leg!"

All turned to look at me. They seemed to be afraid. I hopped away, an omen less graceful than the owl, to the stable loft where I had my roost. There in the straw I fell asleep. The chanting was beginning again in the church.

I awoke later, hearing commotion everywhere below, in the stable and in the minster yard outside. There were men and horses, heavy-footed and chinking with war gear, going to and fro, many torches blazing, and in the stable below me the King himself, already half-dressed in his armor and with a bowl of hot food in his hand. His teeth were chattering. I saw the Earl Cenwulf with him, and old Bishop Humbert, hardly recognizable in his helmet and coat of mail.

"What hour is it now?" asked the King.

"It is showing a gray finger in the east," answered the Bishop. "It will be light in an hour. We have a little time yet, thank God, but none to spare. The host is forming the battle line. All will be well."

"All will be very well," answered the King. "Ah, lord Bishop, ah my thanes, I know it, I know it! While I prayed I saw it clear before my eyes! My heart was filled with it suddenly! A victory, my people! Have faith! Come, I am ready! No, not the helmet yet; I shall go bareheaded. But to horse! I am hot now for the battle and the victory which God will give us!"

His thin face was raised high, his eyes noble, his mouth firm. Here was indeed the tall hero of God. He mounted his horse like a Roman. For a minute longer the yard was full of movement, smoky torchlight flickered on helmets, horses' manes, straps, faces, hauberks, the King's bare head and his arm motioning forward; and a minute later they were all away. They left a sense of sadness behind. A little later the bell began to ring for Prime, that ordinary sound of every morning, which made each morning like the next, and which seemed to be announcing the flat emptiness of all the day ahead.

And flat and empty it was throughout. Could it be possible, we wondered, that somewhere almost within an hour's walk of these our daily tasks, two great armies were drowning the grass in blood to decide the fate of King Edmund and his land? We would stop to listen, expecting to hear, if only now and again, some distant echo of the tumult, a shout, a trumpet; but it was all quietness, made pretty with the small piping of chaffinches from the ricks beyond the hall. Winter sunshine warmed us gently, flocks of high white clouds stood still overhead, and there was not a soul to be seen in the whole countryside except one or two of our monks working in the fields.

Then toward evening one of these, who had been plowing on the far side of the hill near the Roman track, came running over the crest waving his arms to attract our attention. We went to meet him. "There were men going south along the track," he panted as he came up. "Armed men, our people. They were on horseback, hurrying. They said it is all over! They said the heathen are the victors! O Jesu! What are we to do?"

The brethren looked in alarm from one to the other. We found that after all we had not believed that this could happen.

"Brother Esdras has not returned," said someone. Esdras was a monk with a great zeal for fighting the heathen, who had gone with the Prior's blessing to fight beside King Edmund. "Wait till he comes then. The devil sends such alarms as this," said another.

A little while later some men were seen coming slowly over the fields. They carried a wounded man. Prior Ulfwin himself went down and brought them in. They were only a few. They were lost. They named their village, which we had not heard of. Their only anxiety, they said, was to get back there as soon as possible, for their lord, the young man whom they carried, was so deeply wounded they feared he might not live to see his own hall again.

The Abbot gazed down at the young man and peered into his unblinking eyes. "He is already with God," said he.

The men put him down without a word and finding that the Abbot had spoken truly, closed his eyes and wrapped him up in his cloak. Then they began to pray.

"Lord God," said their leader, "if it was Thy will, and for the sins of this land, that the heathen came upon us like a gale of ice upon ripe corn, and beat us down and scattered us, we beg Thee, who were the churls of this man's land, to look with mercy upon his soul. He was Cnebba, lord of the village by the Deep Ford. He spent his blood in Thy battle like a true thane, and held the shield firm for Thee, front, back and side. Receive Thy battle-thane, Lord God."

We gave them food and drink and would have had them stay with us till next morning. If they traveled by night they would risk meeting with wolves along their way.

"There is another kind of wolf we fear more," said they. "Holy fathers, you yourselves had best be away from here before the heathen come. They cannot be far off."

Before they left us, carrying their dead lord between them in his cloak, we asked if they knew what had befallen the King; but they did not.

Alas, before long we learned of this, too. Our few serfs had fled as soon as they could creep away without being seen, and they had left some dogs chained up in one of the huts. Soon after nightfall these dogs began to howl dismally. Looking out to see what was amiss we saw a figure coming over the fields, shadowy and stumbling along the very way King Edmund had come only the day before. My heart went thin with fear, for it was like the King's ghost itself coming to the Judgment of Souls in our church. But it was not; it was Brother Esdras. He came into the hall, where there was a fire, and sat down to warm himself without a word. The brethren asked questions which he hardly appeared to hear and did not answer. In his lap there lay two long arrows, all soaked red with blood. He looked up when Prior Ulfwin came in.

"Father Prior," he said then. "Do you know it all?"

"Not all," replied the Abbot. "What of the King?"

"The heathen took him alive," said Esdras. Then he rose to his feet slowly, and with his head thrown back and his voice loud and chanting, as though he were a bard singing of heroes before the Highest Throne itself, he spoke on. "They took him alive. He would not save himself, the hero of God. They bound him with sharp cords. They dragged him hither and thither like a spoil to be divided, each man fighting his neighbor with baleful greed to lay hands upon the royal prey. Then came the three pagan kings, the sons of Ragnar. 'Tie him to a tree,' they commanded wrathfully from their horses, 'tie him high up, where all can see him.' And so they tied him to a tree. Lo! it was a dead tree, stark and white among the black trees of winter. White also was the Christian king whom they hoisted and bound there. Black Halfdan laughed and shouted aloud: 'Behold the white tree, my vikings! Now let me see how your arrows can paint it red!'"

Esdras paused. He held out the two arrows that he carried, one in each hand, at arm's length. He went on in a low voice.

"The tree became red all down one side. The arrows were thick as pine needles in the forest. These two only I took from the body of the holy martyr when darkness came! Brothers," he cried, raising his voice again, "the holy King Edmund is among the saints tonight, and the very weight of the arrows that sped him there shall at last drag these heathen to hell! Let them despair! That is the victory which was revealed to King Edmund in our church last night!"

The bell did not ring the Offices that night, for the brother whose duty it was to ring it had fled. He was not the only one. Others had already slipped away without taking leave of anyone. The rest spoke openly of going. To stay meant nothing but being roasted alive in the blazing church, as had happened to the monks at Bardeney. But how to go? Should we go all together taking the treasures of the monastery with us, such as they were, perhaps even with a wagon for the heavier gear? But then the pagans would be sure to overtake and rob us. Should we all scatter, each for himself, and hope to reunite in some distant kingdom, in Mercia, or Wessex perhaps, beyond the reach of the pagans? But was any part of England beyond their reach? Who had the strength to stand against them? And here, as it drew toward dawn and we had not yet decided what to do, we began each one of us to feel that heartsick agitation of fear that tingles on the edge of panic. The very fact that we had not seen the heathen at our gate made it the more certain that it could not now be long before they came. For my part I am almost ashamed to think of the terrible trembling that seized me. I found myself suddenly almost too weak to stand. Let it be remembered that I was still only a child. Breathlessly I went to find old Brother Githo. He was in his writing room. One of the big wooden chests stood open, and a hen who usually lived in a heap of straw on top of it was clucking unhappily around Githo's feet. The chest was full of old written scrolls.

"See, boy," said Githo as I came in. "All these scrolls —yet if I ever read one of them I have forgotten it.

What, now, is this?" He picked one out at random; it unrolled stiffly, cracking like an old crust. "It is a poem, a long one. Perhaps it would have been joyful, in the days that I have wasted, to read it and learn what it has had rolled up in its heart all this while. But now it is too late; the heathen are coming to burn it to a cinder. Yet here," he said, "is something they shall not have." He pulled out from the bottom of the chest a great bound book, with a cover of carved wood and clasps of silver. The pages within were filled not only with writing but with little paintings in bright colors. There was gold glittering through the colored, coiled and plaited weavings of pattern that covered every sheet. "It is a lost art," said Githo. "This was done more than a hundred years ago by that same artist who painted the Judgment in the church. There are none like him any more. We have neglected these things, and therefore, truly, we are now little better than the barbarians who are driving us out. However, we will preserve it as a pattern for better times." He began to wrap up the book in a piece of sacking.

"Make haste, Brother Githo," called someone hurrying past the door.

"The Father Prior is to pray with us for the last time, and give us his blessing," said another. "He is already in the church. Come quickly."

"Oh, the delay!" muttered a third, running.

"Tinder!" said Githo, letting the lid fall with a slam over the piled scrolls. "Come, boy, stir your stump. We will go together, you and I."

3

The Heathen

Our leave-taking was hasty. We went in small parties, abandoning our church and rooftree, hardly one of us looking back. We carried little except some food, though one or two of us had taken implements from the farm, an ax, a spade or a hoe. Githo had with him the book wrapped in its sacking and Esdras, who also was with our party, carried, wrapped in a cloth from the altar, the two arrows of King Edmund, on which the blood was already growing dark. It was holy blood, said Esdras; it was dark with vengeance; and, armed with the power of it, the kings of Mercia and Wessex would at last gather their armies and drive the heathen back into the sea.

We went westward toward Mercia. We took the path for Bedricsworth, this very place where now I write and where the body of the martyred Edmund lies now at peace. In those days it was a King's village, and the King himself had a great hall here with finely carved gables and much work in gold.

It was a damp wintry day and we were a forlorn company straggling out along the path. Old Githo with his great book, and I with my crutch, found it hard to keep up with the rest. As we came to the woods at Pakenham we lost sight of them and feared we should soon be left alone, for the others would hardly wait for us. We came up with them again, however, not so much because we had hastened as because they had halted. They stood among the trees at the farther side of the wood gazing toward Bedricsworth, two miles away. From the other side of the low hill beyond which it lay, a cloud of smoke rose up and rolled away southward. Another smaller fire a little to the north of it added its own smoke to the cloud.

"The heathen are there already," said Esdras. "It must be the whole village burning. That to the north would be the King's house."

Confusion now broke out among us. Some were for going on toward Mercia, others were for changing our course and going south. But Esdras spat toward the heathen in Bedricsworth and vowed that with the two arrows of St. Edmund as his only weapon he would go on into Mercia and rouse up King Burgred to drive the accursed heathen out of all the length and breadth of England. So hotly did he speak of it that for a while the rest of us fell warmly in with him. We went on, therefore, keeping among trees and well clear of Bedricsworth, and although we were still close enough to smell the smoke of its burning, we met with no other sign of the enemy. Indeed, I pondered to myself how strange it was that although I had twice in my short lifetime been driven in flight before the oncoming of these terrible men, once as an infant and now again as a boy, yet so far I had never once set eyes upon any of them.

It was growing toward evening and, seeking shelter for the night, we presently came upon a barren place where there were a great number of little huts and wind shelters, mostly made from roughhewn branches, and those that were still in a fair state of repair (for they all had the look of being long neglected) were covered with dried mud and turf. We looked into some of these huts and, finding them empty of all but weeds, decided to stay here till morning. We could not make out what sort of place this was. The huts were very small, only big enough to hold two or three people lying down, and they seemed to be scattered in little groups as far as we could see among the trees and bushes in every direction. Some of us feared that evil spirits might have their abode here, and we therefore took the precaution of making the sign of the cross over the entrances before crawling in.

It was a dismal night! How keenly the wind blew in the crannies, how thin my cloak was, how cold and shuddering was old Githo who lay next to me, and how long it was before I slept! And then almost at once I was aroused by a terrifying howl from the next hut where Esdras lay. A bony creature, who in the moonlight appeared to be no more than a filthy cobbling-together of skins and rags, crawled backward out of the hut and, seeing others of us coming out around him, cried "Mercy!" and crouched there trembling on the ground. It turned out he was a poor bondman whose village had been sacked and whose master's family had all been killed or put into slavery by the heathen, or had run away, he did not know which; he had lived like a wild man in the woods ever since, catching rabbits for food. He had lately been in the habit of sleeping in these huts, but tonight had crawled in upon a living man. In his terror he had shouted out, and it was this that had aroused us all.

He told us what in fact these huts were.

"Why, it was the heathen Danish builded 'em," he said. "They had a camp here, all over through these woods, thousands of 'em, all heathens, big yellow-haired heathens straight from Hell. But ah, good monks, holy men though you be, it must be good to be a heathen man like that when you've got all that strength in your arm!"

We asked if he knew whether there were any heathen between this part of the country and the borders of Mercia.

"Cut, sack, burn, drink and swipe," said he. "They're all over the land, these devils, but between here and Mercia it's the very mouth of Hell, as you might say. Don't go that way, holy monks, or they'll cut off your heads if they catch you. With my own eyes I saw one once who had a monk's head in a bird cage, hanging at his saddle. It was like a pudding."

Before that wretched night was over, sitting in the cold, for we had no means to light a fire and we could not sleep, most of our party forsook the Mercian road and decided to go southward in the morning. Yet Esdras would not change, and neither for some reason would Githo; and I could not part from Githo. As soon as it was light we separated, the others going southward, we three continuing toward the road-town of Cambridge on the borders of Mercia.

Our small supply of food was now being used up. We had hoped to receive alms at the villages on our way, to help us, but we wandered in the woods for many hours without seeing any dwelling until we came to a great heath, and here not far from the wood was a small village with a church. I thought I saw some men at the corner of one of the houses, but when we came to it we found the whole place ransacked and deserted. Doors hung off their hinges, and floors within were all mud under the caved-in thatch, a wooden platter had rolled from a table and lay half-floating in a puddle; in one hut lay the flyblown carcass of a sheep, in another a few broken pots, and nothing stirred anywhere except an old rag flapping in the rubbish on the floor of the roofless church. We spoke with lowered voices.

"The only men here are in the cemetery," said Githo; but even as he spoke there appeared for a moment among some huts a short distance away the men I had seen before. That they saw us was certain, but they moved out of sight again at once, behind the huts. After a moment Esdras called out:

"Who is there? We here are none but two monks and a boy. We are unarmed. We do not come to rob, and have nothing ourselves worth robbing. We are hungry and come to beg food."

At first there was no answer at all, but we stood still and after a minute a swarthy man appeared around a nearby corner.

Esdras asked, "Do you live here? Can you give us food?"

The man shook his head and said, "Not here. No one lives here."

"Is there anyone near?" asked Esdras.

"There is a dead man," said the other. "Can you say the Christian prayers for him? You say you are a monk."

"Did he die in peace?" asked Esdras.

"Who knows? We found him here and buried him. We came to see what we could pick up, but it's all been looted before, not so much as a knife handle left for us, and all we found was this dead man. We were afraid his ghost might haunt us, seeing we had found him unburied; so we buried him, but we don't know the prayers to keep him in his grave. If you are a priest and can say the prayers over him, we will give you food. If not, you can starve."

"And if we do not say the prayers," replied Esdras angrily, "and if this man's ghost cleaves to you and brings you bad luck wherever you go, what will you do then, fool? And how do I know he was a Christian? I cannot pray over a heathen grave."

"The heathen always bury their own kind," the man replied. "This was some fellow who was killed at his hearth when the heathen came. It must have been several months ago. The sea thieves came this way from the fens. They carried the people off to their ships and sold them as slaves overseas. There are many such empty places as this, about here."

The second man, who had evidently been listening nearby, now joined his companion, and together they led the way to a hut where in the floor they had dug the villager's grave. They stood outside and waited while Esdras and Githo together went in and said the necessary prayers. They looked at me and my crutch. Almost with envy one of them said:

"A beggar could do well for himself like that. Going from one fat monastery to the next upon one leg, that's the way to live!"

When Githo and Esdras came out of the hut the men bade us follow them and led us away from the village and over the heath for about an hour's walking. At the end of this time we came to a great rampart, an ancient earthwork all grown over with grass. It stretched across the heath as far as one could see, from north to south. We climbed over it, and on the other side there was a ditch, as deep as the mound was high, and down in this hollow there were a number of people, men and women and some children, about a dozen altogether, with as many cows, some sheep and goats, and two or three horses. There was a fire and a pot boiling over it, and the smell of food. The swarthy man, our leader, called out:

"Here you are, I've brought you nothing this time but some mouths to feed. Feed them quickly and let them go."

But after we had been fed a dispute arose whether we should go or not; for one of the women had a newborn baby that had to be christened, and one of the older men was elf-shotten in the small of his back and could not bend for pain, and needed prayers, and others thought it bad luck to send away a priest or a monk. And when they learned that we were going toward Mercia as they were themselves, they at last decided, with some reluctance from the swarthy man and his companion, that we should go along with them.

We learned that these people had been wandering for many weeks. Most of them were free churls who had been dispossessed by the plundering Danes; at least that is what they said, but in the world as it was then it was not wise to look too closely into such things. They might equally have been runaway serfs who had become outlaws, plundering again the already plundered land. The cattle, they said, were their own, which they were driving away so that the heathen should not have them, but who was to say that they were not stolen from men who now lay dead around King Edmund's banner? They were driving them to sell in the peaceful country beyond Cambridge town.

Once more it drew on toward evening. It was decided to camp for the night where we were. The fire was built up for the night in the shelter of the great ditch, where it could not be seen from any distance. A sentry was posted on the bank above. Those who could not get near enough to the fire—and we, Githo, Esdras and I were among them—were advised to lie for warmth among the sheep; which we did, though whether that is good advice or not I cannot say, for I was so tired the sheep might have rolled on me and I would not have wakened to care. Before we slept, Brother Githo baptized the baby.

We were roused at first light by a great kicking and commotion. "Up, up, up! On your feet. On the march. Up, up, up! It is dawn."

It was dark. It was cold. We marched hungry. My crutch was heavy. My teeth chattered. I could not keep up with the others over the rough ground. I stumbled and rose and tried to go faster. I wept openly for the shame and the haste and the despair and the dismal gray of the windy grass in half-light. The woman with the baby called out, "What's the hurry? Must we all break our necks at this time of the morning? I've twice nearly pitched over with my foot in these rabbit holes."

The swarthy man said, "Move, move. Stop your clacking and save your breath. There are strange horsemen about. I saw them myself, riding in the dawn about a mile off. Who knows what they are? Keep moving."

We had followed the course of the long dike, keeping in the ditch so far as we could, and by the time it was full light we came to the end of it. Here was a river, a cold and weedy branch of the fens, and here we turned westward along its bank, still toward Cambridge. We went over rough fields, all neglected. Then at last I had to pause. I could not keep up any longer on my crutch. "Let them go on without us," said Githo. "What difference does it make? Esdras and I will stay with you."

"Can he sit one of our horses?" asked the swarthy man, looking back impatiently.

I said I thought I could.

"Horses! Horses!" a voice shouted suddenly in alarm. "Look over there!" In confusion, wondering what this could be, I looked where the man was pointing, back to the dike which we had left but which could still be seen as a ridge on the horizon. Between it and ourselves a dark line of moving shapes was approaching us over the fields. They were men on horseback, coming at a steady trot and spreading out to head us off and close in on us with our backs to the marshy river which was too wide to cross.

"The heathen! Holy Mother protect us, they are the heathen!" cried a woman next to me. Her child, a little girl, clung close against her. "Holy Mother protect us!" murmured the woman, sinking to her knees and making the sign of the cross.

For a moment one or two of our men looked as though they were prepared to make a fight of it, others as if they would try to escape on the two or three horses we had; but a moment's judgment soon showed there was no hope in either course. The oncoming Danes must have numbered more than thirty, all well-armed and mounted, and their wide semicircle, now completely around us, was moving in at a walking pace.

Man for man they seemed bigger than the English. They were fair-haired and red-faced. I noticed that some of them had bracelets and other pieces of jewelry, and some had embroidered cloaks, but for the most part there was no great show of stolen luxury about them such as I had expected. Indeed they had a rather plain, working-day appearance as they trotted up laughing and talking among themselves. We all stood hemmed in and waiting, doing nothing. Two or three of the heathen rode forward and began to drive away our cattle without a word to us. We offered no resistance. The leader of the Danes, a huge man wearing a coat all sewn over with iron plates, laughed and called out:

"Hola, dog English! Ye be cattle thieves, hey? Dost thou go to slink off sidling, hey? Dost thou go creeping? Thou shalt creep on all fours now, shalt thou not? Hoi! Dog English cattle thieves, what else hast thou stolen, ye dirty jackdaw-men? What else have ye hid among your lice, hey? Strip, strip, off clothes, off."

The women they drove off to one side with the cattle, and the rest of us were made to strip. The heathen took anything of the least value they could find in our clothes, while we stood shivering naked in the bitter wind. I was surprised to find how much stuff there was. Our swarthy man and his companion had found plenty in their own looting; but Githo and Esdras and myself gave promise of little enough. Esdras' two arrows caused some interest, and I knew Esdras was ready in his heart to die before he would part with them; but fortunately some other thing distracted the raiders —I think it was because at that moment they discovered my one-leggedness to which they all paid a wondering and rather benevolent attention for some minutes. It may have been by a miracle that the red arrows went unnoticed after that. But then, alas, at the bottom of Githo's sack, where it had lain hidden in its dirty wrapping since we left Thornham, one of them discovered the great book. The finder held it up and opened it at a page which was marvelously colored. His companions crowded around to see. Poor Githo covered his face with his hands and muttered, "God, O Lord, let them not take it! It cannot be of any worth to them. Let them give back what they cannot understand!"

It was true enough. They could not understand it, and they presently began to suspect it had little value. There was a gabbling crowd of argument, hands were thrusting in, pulling this way and that, and then there was a sound of tearing, for the pages were old and brittle.

"No!" Githo cried, and shouldered his way into the crowd, panting. "No, no! Do not tear it!"

The pagans looked first astonished at his passion, then began to laugh. One of them deliberately tore out a page and wagged it in his face. A roar of laughter followed as Githo with tears rolling down his face tried to reach the book. Another page was torn out, and another. Then the one who held it called out, "Look see, old man, thou go get!" and he flung the book over their heads, out with a splash into the middle of the river. Old Githo stood silent, mouth open, naked, a poor old figure of despair, staring at the ripples on the water.

"Thou go get!" the heathen shouted, laughing, and two of them suddenly seized and lifted him head high and flung him into the icy water.

A roar of laughter went up.

"Swim, swim, all swim!" they cried, and on the spur of the moment with spears and kicks and much laughing they began to drive all of us into the river.

"All swim, all swim!" they shouted as the last one splashed among the reeds. The victims stood up to their necks, blue with cold and pricked back at the spear's point whenever they tried to clamber out. Only the women and children and myself did they exempt from this game. "Not thee, thou little one-leg, not thee," said one of them to me, and he smiled and patted me on the back.

A short while after, their leader, who had been away looking over the cattle, rode up, and after joining in the laughter at this sport, presently put two fingers in his mouth and gave a loud whistle.

"To horse now, my vikings!" he ordered. "Away hoi! Hoi, away!"

With hardly a look back at their victims who were at last free to clamber and haul each other out of the water into the November wind, the pagans got on their horses and began to ride off, driving the cattle at a casual pace, talking and laughing among themselves, just as they had come.

They had left the women and children—whether out of mercy, or because they could not at that time be bothered to take away such cattle as these, there was no saying, but leave them they did. These now came running to help the poor teeth-chattering wretches who dragged themselves up the muddy bank. The Danes had taken most of their clothes. We who were dry took off some of ours and gave them. Even the stern Esdras could hardly drag his sinewy body along because of shivering, yet before he would dry or dress himself he went and found those two arrows which had become for him a symbol of vengeance and deliverance. Poor Githo did not speak, but shuddered all the while as we helped him along. Dressed thus in odds and ends of each other's torn garments we stumbled slowly along until by God's mercy we at last found a swineherd's shack where there was a fire; and here, with the swineherd wishing us nothing but ill-hap and good riddance, we stayed until clothes and bodies were dry, and life and feeling and the beginnings of warmth had begun to return once more.

The next day we reached the town of Cambridge, a wretched place whose lord, a traitor, had fled with his family to the protection of the Danes, and whose few remaining inhabitants were little better than the heathen whom they were themselves quite ready to serve. Here we left our companions, and went on, the three of us, into Mercia. Poor Githo coughed and shivered all the way. After several days of wandering we at last found shelter at a monastery near the village of Bedford. Here poor Githo became ill and took to his bed.

4

The Crutch and the Harness

We stayed many months in the monastery at Bedford, and all the while Githo's illness grew worse. It was clear he could not live much longer. All the while, too, we were hearing news of that other illness which was ravaging our homeland of East Anglia. The destroyers spent that year plundering it and picking it clean, while at the same time they sharpened their swords for a new conquest when this was eaten up; and all the while, too, they were being joined by fresh shiploads of their countrymen from Denmark, eager for a share of the next adventure. But we heard nothing of any mustering of Christian armies in Mercia to oppose them.

There was a well-born monk at Bedford who was a friend of Ceowulf the Ealdorman, lord of that part of Mercia; he professed to know the things that went on in the minds of the lords and bishops in King Burgred's hall. His name was Oswy. Esdras asked him one day if there was any preparation being made against the Danes. Oswy replied with a shrug that he had not heard of any need for it.

"But, brother," said Esdras, "here is a Christian land in peril, while Christian men are smiling and twiddling their thumbs."

Oswy smiled and stopped twiddling his thumbs, and he replied, "Brother, there is no peril. The Danes, if they march, will not march this way. King Burgred knows who are his enemies." He smiled again knowingly, and winked, and then pointed away toward the south. "Over that way, in Wessex," he said, "are the worst enemies of Mercia. And," he added with another wink, "that is the way the Danes will march. Not here, not this way."

"But," said Esdras, "if Wessex and Mercia would fight as allies together they could drive the heathen into the sea."

"The men of Wessex are ferocious enough to do it alone," said Oswy. "Let them try. If they succeed or if they fail, both they and the Danes will have had enough of fighting by the time they've finished with each other. And when they've broken each other's teeth and knocked each other's eyes out, that will be time for Mercia to blow the war horn. It is forty years since Egbert of Wessex made our kings of Mercia his vassals. We have an old score to pay."

Esdras then questioned him about the kings of Wessex.

"It is said that the family of Egbert is under a curse," said Oswy. "Egbert himself was strong, but it was in his day that the heathen first began to raid our coasts. His son, they say, was a weak king and a sinful man. And his grandsons . . ." He made an expression of contempt. "There were four grandsons of Egbert, four brothers. Two have already died wearing the crown of Wessex. The third is Ethelred, who wears it today. And when the Danes have finished with him, there will remain only the last, the youngest brother, a poor creature cursed with an incurable sickness, who, they say, is taken up with piety and book reading. He is called Alfred. He is no sort of man to be a king."

This was the first we heard of Alfred, noblest of kings, England's deliverer.

A dream came to me one night. I dreamed that I felt something touch me on the shoulder and heard a dry voice call me by my name, "Alfred!" I sat up in my bed of straw, but saw nothing except my crutch leaning against the wall. I lay down again, but I felt the tap on my shoulder, and the dry voice: "Alfred!" I said, "Who is it? Where are you?" and the voice answered, "You can see me"; but I could see nothing but the crutch. "You can see me," said the voice again, and I knew it was my crutch which spoke to me. "What do you want?" I asked. The crutch said, "Get out of your bed and let me lie in it. Why should you lie sleeping at ease whilst I lean against the wall all night—I who am the master of us two?"

"Insolent crutch!" I cried. "You are nothing but

my servant. I will break you in half, I will burn you and get another." "I am your Crutch, be it one crutch or another," answered the thing, "and you will always go at what pace I tell you, and no other. You will crawl under my weight. I will always be the master and you the servant, because you cannot do without the sop I bring you, the food of your nature—the soft food called Pity!" At this I cried out, and seizing the crutch I flung it out at the door, and fell to weeping in my sleep. When I awoke next morning I saw that the crutch was lying outside the door of my cell. A monk who was passing by stooped and picked it up, and brought it in to me with a kind smile.

The next night I had the same dream again, but this time I was unable to fling the crutch out of the door because as I seized it, it took root in the ground before me and stood so firm that I could not even shake it. The third night it happened again; but this time when I lifted the crutch to throw it away, it wrenched itself out of my hand and began to beat me on the head and shoulders until I cried aloud with pain. I awoke at once and found that my back was sore and painful, and the crutch was lying across my bed as if it had just fallen there. I stood up then on my one leg in the middle of the hut and supported myself against the roof post with my hand, and cried out:

"O Lord God, must I be always the servant of this misfortune you have put upon me?"

Then I thought I heard a voice speaking to me, as though it were sounding upon a harpstring stretched inside my head. The voice said:

"There are three ways with misfortune. You may be its servant; you may be its equal; or you may be its master. The first you will have if you weep for it; the second you will have if you take no heed of it; the third you will have only if you can learn from the thing you hold in your hand. Take it and show it to your namesake."

In one hand I held nothing; with the other I supported myself against the roof post. Then I felt with this hand and found that under it, hanging against the roof post, was something that appeared to be made of straps. I took it down and hopped with it to the door and examined it in the moonlight. It was an old horse harness: bit, headstall and reins.

From time to time we had news of the heathen army in East Anglia. There had been changes. Some of the chieftains and their crews had left them and taken to the sea again; but others, many more, had come to take their places. Among these was the ferocious King Bacsec, with a great following, and Sidroc the Jarl, plunderer of all the Seine valley in Frankland, with his bloodthirsty son.

"These are men to make the fleas jump about in Wessex," said Oswy.

"And you still do not think they will march this way?" said Esdras.

"We have their word for it," said Oswy.

"It is not the word of Christian men," replied Esdras. He said no more till the other had gone; then he spoke bitterly. "The men of this kingdom are all blind

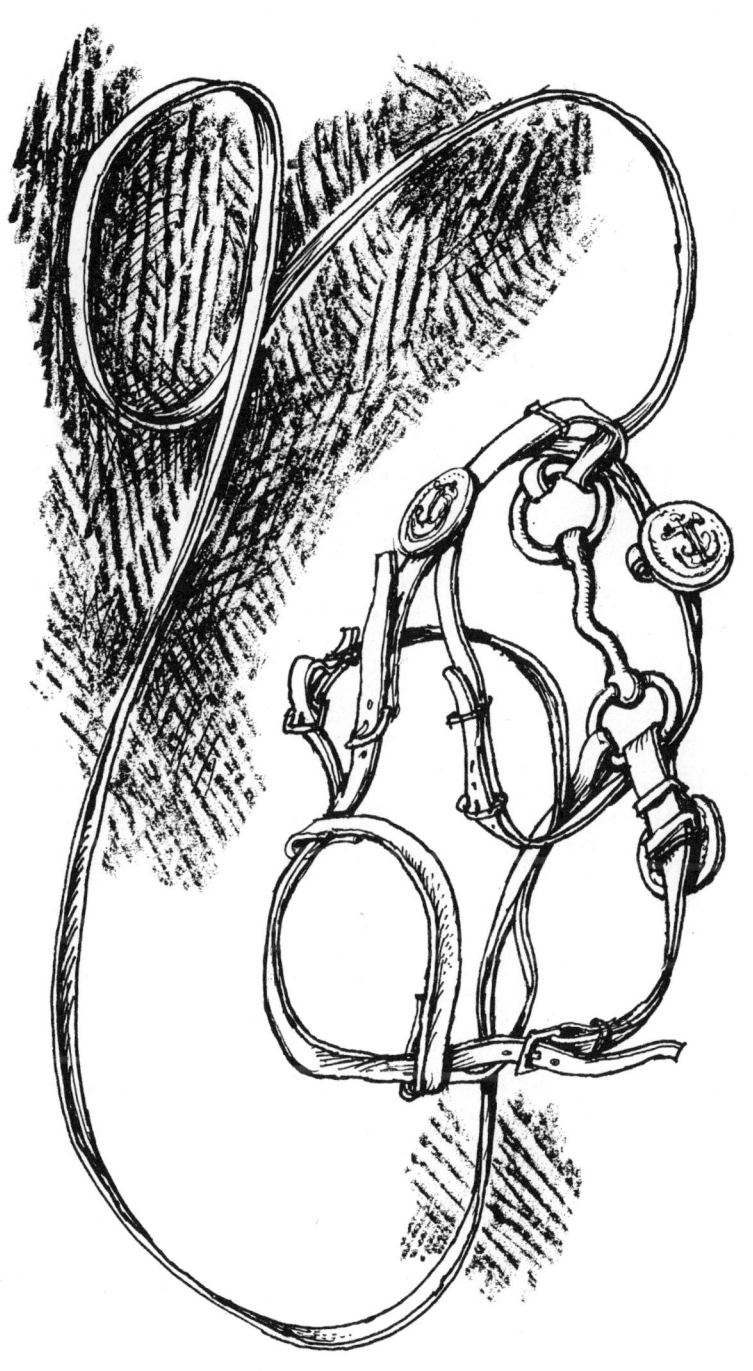

in the folly of their fatness. They stand like silly sheep with a wise look, cunningly instructing the butcher in the art of sharpening knives. I will leave this place. I would rather take what risks there are to be taken in Wessex, where men are prepared to take them standing up, than wait here in Mercia, which will certainly go down before the heathen, not with a great fall, but sagging at the knees."

But he did not go at once, though it was now summertime and the roads good for traveling, because it was clear that old Githo was dying. We three had come from Thornham together and were without kin in a distant country, and Esdras said that he would wait awhile and not leave the old man to die alone.

I was troubled about my dream. I spoke of it to Esdras and showed him the harness. I repeated what the voice had said to me: "Go and show it to your namesake."

"Alfred," said Esdras. "It is a name that is heard often enough. But there is no one here of that name."

I said, "It is the name of the King's brother in Wessex. Could it be he?"

Esdras looked hard at me. He said, "Is this a thought that stays with you?"

I answered, "It stays with me. I have prayed about it, as I have been taught to do; and the thought stays with me, night and day."

Then said Esdras, "Which way have you chosen? Will you be the servant, the equal, or the master?"

I said, "I will be the master if I can."

"If so," said Esdras, "you must take the harness to

Alfred of Wessex. We will go together, for I also have a gift to give. I will take the two arrows of King Edmund and give them to the King of Wessex, Alfred's brother."

Old Githo died just before Christmas, and was buried at the monastery. Then at the beginning of the New Year, Esdras and I said our farewell to Bedford and set out together for Wessex. When we joined the road called the Icknield Way, which leads down into Wessex from East Anglia, we found it all trampled and littered with signs of a great army which had passed that way not many days before, going in the same direction. The heathen had gone before us.

5

The First Blow in Wessex

THESE HEATHEN were a sea army waging war on land. Though they now went on horseback they were still the same ships' companies that had pulled at the oars together in the long dragon-galleys, and their jarls were the same viking captains who had commanded them at sea. Their method of warfare was the same, whether they harried from the sea among the salt creeks, or inland among the hills and forests. It is true they usually did not like to be long away from their ships; but these were of such shallow draft that they could be rowed far inland up the rivers, as all the great river valleys of the world between the mouths of the Rhine and the savage rims of the Black Sea, and all the great cities between Paris and Byzantium, knew to their cost. The heathen would beach their ships in twos and threes, or in twenties and thirties, in a green countryside, and build a great stockade around them; and from this they would sally out to plunder, till there was nothing left in the land for miles around but the stalk, the husk and the empty shell. From their stockades, if anyone dared to attack them, which was rare, and if they became so hard pressed they could not defend the place, which was rarer still, they had only to launch their ships and row away; and on water there was nothing to oppose them in the whole of Christendom.

So now in Wessex, galloping under the Black Raven, the banner of Odin, they worked to the same plan. They did not come by water, because there were not ships enough to carry an army so numerous as they had now become, but they made for the rivers none the less, knowing that when they had built a fort, other ships, coming from Denmark in the summer months, would bring further armies to join them.

Their march was swift. The folk in the villages along their way had no warning before the first galloping men went through, pausing only to get information about the road ahead and send back a rider to the vanguard of the main army, which soon began to invade field and village on all sides, like the coming of a flood. The folk fled to the woods, and the Wessex men, with shield, spear and ax, gathered around their war leaders. Ethelwulf, the Ealdorman of Berkshire, sent out his war horn to muster them. His messengers took the news to Ethelred the King.

The village of Reading lies at a point where many

streams and valleys come down to the River Thames. Here, on a dark morning, the vanguard of the heathen army galloped in. Half of the people had already fled, being warned of their approach, and the remainder were already driving out their oxen when Halfdan's men cut them off. They did not much hinder the people—indeed they drove out those who still remained; but oxen, fowl, goods and gear, meat and grain, hearth and home, these they took for themselves. They knew well what they were about, and some said that Mercian spies who knew the country had guided them to this place, from which the whole of northeastern Wessex lay open to their pillage. Here on a tongue of land where the Kennet joins the Thames they had short work to make themselves secure with a palisade after their usual manner, and in and around the village itself their own huts sprang up in clustered hundreds, looking among the village houses like toadstools in a garden of beehives. In the Reeve's house, and in all the bigger houses of the place, their kings and chiefs set themselves up. There were not barns or granaries enough for their needs, however. Seeking more space, several of them entered the church, and there they saw a figure of Christ on His cross upon the altar. They withdrew respectfully, considering it wise to be cautious with other men's gods, and reported the matter to Halfdan.

He said, "Cast Christ into the river and let Him swim."

But Jarl Guthorm said, "Be careful, in case this god has some power over the water in these parts. If by any chance He could bring down a flood upon us we should be soon swimming here ourselves. Let us give Him a boat to go in."

So they made a little boat and put the Christ in it and launched it upon the Thames; and when it had floated out of sight they entered the church and defiled it by putting up their own gods, made of straw and wood, in a row upon the altar; and the rest of the church they used as a storehouse for their plunder.

On the third day, while most of their army was still busy digging the rampart between the two rivers, about fifty of them led by the jarls Sidroc and Guthorm sallied out on horseback to forage along the river toward Newbury. After about six miles they came to a place called Englefield, which lies in the shelter of a wooded hill. When they got there they heard among the trees on the hillside a noise like the lowing of a herd of cattle. There was also an old woman in a red kirtle who was hurrying as fast as she could to reach the shelter of the trees farther up the slope. They called to her, but she only went the faster.

"Old mother," shouted Sidroc the Jarl. "Thou hadst best turn about and answer us, or this is the last day's light thou shalt ever see."

At this she halted and turned about, and shouted back to them in a loud voice:

"You swine's tripe! I am blind already, and I thank God I do not share the daylight with such as you. But I still have my nose; and with that I can smell the dunghill under which your father buried your father's father. Go now, dung-pigs, and dig him up!" And with that she ran still higher among the trees.

"Fetch her down!" shouted Jarl Sidroc. "Fetch her down, and all the other cattle I hear bellowing up there in the trees! And by the hammer of Thor I'll roast that old woman over the same fire that roasts her oxen!"

They all spurred forward up the slope; but at the same moment there flew an arrow from the trees, and then another, and then a score; Jarl Sidroc tumbled headlong from his saddle and all the horses turned this way and that in confusion. Before they could dismount, the pagans saw bright shields in the wood, and heard the war horns of Ethelwulf and the Wessex men.

"Back!" shouted Guthorm. "It is a trap! Back and dismount on level ground! We cannot fight here on the slope!"

But some had already dismounted and had begun to form a shield-wall where they stood, while others were already going back; and while they were thus confused, Ethelwulf and his thanes came down upon them with spears and axes and sharp swords. The Danes fought bravely and long in spite of their confusion, but they were too few for the Wessex men, and in the end they turned and fled with what horses they had left back to their camp, leaving Sidroc the Jarl lying dead on the field.

This was the first blow of the West Saxons. The heathen at once sent out strong forces from their camp to test the strength of the enemy, but this time they found none; for Ethelwulf still had none but his own Berkshire men, too few to risk a pitched battle. He had withdrawn therefore toward Newbury, and there, two days later, King Ethelred and his brother, the lord Alfred, with the King's thanes and the ealdormen of Wiltshire and Hampshire and all their battle thanes and freemen, joined them. With this army they advanced once more upon Reading.

The Danes had set up outposts on the ridge of the hills west of Tilehurst, about four miles from their camp, and from here they saw the sun flashing upon the spears of the West Saxons among the trees of the valley. So rapidly did these advance that the Danish outposts could not withdraw but were obliged to stand and offer fight, making out by a cunning show among the trees that they were more numerous than they truly were, so as to delay the Wessex men, while the pagans from the great camp had time to arm themselves and form up for battle; so, when the outposts had been driven back and King Ethelred advanced, he found the great army waiting for him on the level ground before the camp.

There the West Saxons struck their second blow; and there, after great bloodshed, they were defeated. They did not spare their valor, but nevertheless they were driven back. In the evening, after the long day, they were forced to fly from the field, with the victorious war horns of the heathen hunting them through the woods. The Saxon dead lay strewn all around, and a cold rain rained down upon them; and among them, dead in the rain, lay the valiant Ethelwulf, Ealdorman of Berkshire. It was a bad day and a black night.

6

The King's Brother

Esdras and I followed the road from Bedford in the tracks of the heathen army. The mud, which had been trodden into ridges by their horses' hooves, had now frozen hard and made rough going for us both, but especially for me with my crutch. Esdras, I believe, noticed nothing of it, either the rough road, the cold, or my struggling to keep up with him; he now cared for nothing but to reach Wessex and to join battle with the heathen as quickly as he could. His burning mood was on him. He was a man of zeal. In his heart there dwelt an angel of bloodshed, like the angel that destroyed the firstborn of the Egyptians, and when this angel began to rage and speak to him, as now it did, his eyes looked strange and he appeared not to see familiar things.

But my crutch chafed and chafed. All the way Esdras strode ahead, and I humped along after him on my cold foot, until sometimes I had to call out to him to stop. Then he would wait for me with a sort of patient impatience, like one who suffers a private penance that has to be endured without being spoken of. But once when I was so tired that I had to stop and sit down, and Esdras saw I was on the point of weeping, he suddenly became gentle and knelt by me and began to rub my foot to bring back the warmth. Then he lifted me up and helped me along till we found a place where some of the Danes had had a campfire not long before, and deep down in the ash there were a few embers which Esdras with patience and dry twigs was able to coax into a flame. But I ached all over and was in such low spirits I could not enjoy even the warmth. I flung the harness away from me as far as I could into the bushes, and wept. Esdras looked sternly at me.

"Why do you fling aside your harness?" he asked. "Do you not remember your dream? Was it not said that only from the harness would you learn to master your crutch?"

"In my dream, the crutch said I would always go at a crutch's pace," I answered miserably, "and it was true, Esdras. I can go no faster. And the harness is only another burden."

Esdras said, "A harness is the sign of cunning work. By the work and skill it takes to make it and to put it on, a noble spirit in a weak body can control the strong but unskilled brute; and even the brute which wears it can then share the greater dignity of his master. If the Lord God puts His harness upon you, will you throw it away? Will you refuse to learn your lesson or to finish your task? It is true that if you cease to strain and pull, you can always have your crutch to lean upon. But who, then, is the master?"

I answered, "Oh, Esdras, the crutch is my master. Go on, and leave me here!"

"There indeed speaks the crutch!" replied Esdras, scornfully. "Hark how it whimpers! How it begs for my pity! And shall I, then, leave you alone in this wild road to come on at your own pace as best you can? And shall I not hear the wolves howling in the woods, hungry for the one-legged boy? No, I will not leave you. But if you cannot carry your own burden, you shall feel that you are nothing but a burden to me, be sure of that! Come, get up now and we will go on."

In my heart I knew he had spoken the truth. I put down my foot upon my self-pity, gave him my hand and rose up. At that moment we heard a sound among the bushes nearby, and turning, saw coming toward us a brown pony. It had a saddle, though the girth had slipped, but it was without a bridle. It came and stood near at hand, cropping the grass; and the harness which I had flung away lay almost at its feet.

Esdras went and picked up the harness and handed it to me without a word. I took it and put it over the pony's head. It stood patiently while I struggled to adjust the old hard leather and the buckles, stiff with being long out of use. But at last it was done. We tightened the saddle girth and shortened the stirrup leather, and then Esdras helped me to mount.

"Now," he said, "sit steadily and I will lead you. You see that the Lord God did not send you a harness for nothing."

I laughed. "You spoke very finely about that," I said, "but you had it the wrong way round, Esdras. You never thought of it this way."

"This is a harness which works both ways," said Esdras.

We guessed that the pony was one which had broken away from the march of the Danish army; or perhaps they had driven it away as being useless, for it was an old beast and gentle, hardly suitable for them in their tumultuous march along the Chiltern Hills. But for my needs it was heaven-sent.

Between the Chilterns and the Berkshire Hills our way led us down to a valley through which the River Thames runs southward toward Reading. Here the tracks of the heathen army turned south also, following the river. The frost had thawed now, and a chilly rain, which had been falling since the previous evening, had turned the path into a slop of mud. Through this, on the other bank of the river, we saw from a distance long files of men and horses trudging slowly northward and away from us along the lee of the Berkshire Hills. Others were coming on our side of the stream looking for a ford.

"These are not Danes, but English," muttered Esdras. "What has happened here? It looks like misfortune."

At the ford, wretched in the rain, there were three

wounded men. Esdras helped them to cross, and asked what had happened. They answered in the strong accent of the West Saxons: "A battle, yesterday, down there. Ai, the chopping! I never did see butcher's work to beat it! God helping us, we wounded ones had to creep away in the dark on our hands and knees, and it were hours before we found Saxon folk again, they'd all fled so fast and so far. Ai, what a trouncing we had! The heathen is a very scourge from the Lord God, so says our priest, and truly do I believe it. We weren't meant to fight against 'em, but to endure 'em as a scourge! And that's endurance upon endurance, so it is!"

"And where are you going now?" asked Esdras.

"How do we know that, father monk? We've been following the rest, that's all. What's more, if we don't hasten, they'll leave us behind, and then where'll we be? Our men have been going past here all day, and now there's only the stragglers coming up, like us."

Soon after, a pair of oxen dragging a farm cart came along at a mud-slithering pace, goaded by an old peasant. The cart was already full of wounded, but room was found for these other three, and with them the oxen plodded on.

In the afternoon the rain clouds cleared, leaving holes of blue sky big enough to encourage a few birds to sing. We saw no more soldiers until we came to a village sheltered among trees, under the lee of the downs. Here, around a big fire in the open, there were some twenty or thirty men who appeared to be all of one company. Some were drying their clothes, and some were cooking meat on the points of their spears. There was a dispute going on among them.

It appeared they were all Sussex men, from the other side of the Forest of Andred. They had come with their lord, the Ealdorman, to fight for his overlord, the King of Wessex. But in the flight after the battle they had lost sight of the Ealdorman's standard because of the darkness. Some said they had seen the standard-bearer following the main body of the Wessex men going to the north; others that their own people had gone south, back toward Sussex; and others again had heard that the Ealdorman himself had been killed and the standard carried off by the Danes. At all events they were now leaderless and did not know where their loyalty lay. Some held that it belonged to the King's army, but most were of the opinion that they ought to go back to defend their own lands in Sussex.

"We don't owe loyalty to any army, but only to our own lord," said one. "We have stood by him in the shield-wall like true men. Many of us have shed our blood along with his. That is the law of our fathers and of our sons, and we have willingly done all we could. But now if our lord is dead, we must go back to serve his heirs and our own farmsteads. It is our duty, and no one can do it for us if we fail in it."

While they were arguing in this way, two men came up on horseback and reined in to listen. One of them was broad and clean-shaven, with a beaky nose and shaggy eyebrows. He was clad in a massive coat of iron scales. He had an ax and a great sword, and his helmet, which hung at his saddle, was of the heavy Frankish type. The other man was younger. He had a lean face, with a small fair beard. He was without armor, and he wore a cap of fur.

The armored man, speaking from his horse in a commanding voice, asked what the argument was about. Being told, he cried:

"By God's Chair! Go home, then, if you must! But how do you suppose you can reach your own lands without first fighting your way through the whole heathen army, who are more numerous than you could dream of in a lifetime of nightmares? Try it, if you wish, and God's strength be with you! But if you are so bent upon fighting, you would do best to stay with us and fight another battle for the King."

"We are not afraid of battles," said they, "but who is to make amends to our families, and who is to speak for us when our blood-money is shared out, if we die fighting under a strange banner for a lord who does not know us and whom we do not know?"

Then the other man rode forward and taking off his fur cap so that his whole head could be clearly seen, he said:

"Look at me. Will you know me, and will you fight under my banner until you find your own lord again? I am Alfred of Wessex, the King's brother. I will remember you, and I myself will speak for your blood-price when the time comes, if you will fight with my men under my flag."

This, then, was how I first saw my namesake. I remember thinking how like any ordinary man he looked, except for the leanness of his face which made him look older than his years. He was then twenty-one years of age. He was of middle height. His clothes were plain; indeed he seldom wore embroidery, or any extravagance of ornament, though he liked to show his high birth by wearing finely woven stuffs and well-washed linen. Today, however, he looked no different from any other soldier, in his rough cloak, wet from the rain. "Well," he said to the Sussex men who had all taken off their caps and were even, some of them, going down on their knees in the mud. "Well, have you decided? And do not kneel; you kneel to God and your bishop, not to me. If you will serve me, serve me on your feet. Well?" His horse was growing restless.

"Yes, King-born, yes, we will serve you," said the men.

"Good. And I will pay my part of the bargain. Now, Guntram, stay and show them the way. Put them with Cerdic's men. They must be there before nightfall. Tell Cerdic. Follow after me as soon as you can. I am going back now; my horse needs to gallop and I have matters waiting for me at the camp."

He wheeled his horse around, and galloped off. The knight Guntram wheeled also and went a little way after him, shouting:

"My lord, you must not ride alone!"

But he had no reply from the galloping figure, and so turned back again toward the Sussex men, who were already picking up their gear, ready to be off.

"And just for you," he said, "I am ordered to forget my first duty, and let him ride alone, without escort. Listen to me, then, you: That was the noble lord

Alfred, and I, Guntram the Frank, am his sword-bearer, and there is not one of you whom I would not see chopped into small pieces before I would let harm come to him. And may God grant that none does come to him between here and his tent, for that's a bad horse he has, and I told him not to ride it, but he will have his own way. To serve him is hard work, as you will soon find. Now, then, how many are there of you...?"

In a very short while he had them ready for the march, instructed them where to find Cerdic, to whose banner they were going, and turned again to ride off. But the hand of the monk Esdras was on his bridle. "Let go!" the knight exclaimed. "I have not time for more of you!"

Esdras said, "Not so fast. I have something here for the King, and this boy has a message for Alfred, your lord. Tell us now where we can find them."

Guntram said, "What sort of madman are you? You have the dress of a monk and the manner of an assassin. What have you for the King?"

"I bring him two arrows taken from the body of the holy martyr Edmund, last king of the East Angles," said Esdras. "They are a sign from the God of Vengeance, against the enemy, for their great crime."

Guntram crossed himself and said, "I have heard of that terrible thing. But first tell me how you came to have these arrows; and what has this boy for the lord Alfred?"

While Esdras told him, the knight Guntram looked

hard at me and at my empty stirrup. When Esdras' account was finished, he said:

"I am no judge of these holy matters. May God forgive me, I have sometimes thought that if we Christians spent less time in praying for miracles to help us we might have more time to help ourselves. But the lord Alfred says this is like blasphemy, God forgive me. As for you, the Bishop of Sherborne is your man; he can decide what you're good for. I will take you to him if you can ride the boy's mount. And the boy can ride up here in front of me."

So we rode the last few miles, Esdras jolting along on my pony, myself aloft on the saddlebow of the warhorse of Guntram the Frank.

7

King Ethelred

ALONG THE road, among the trees, in open fields, in the hollows and up the steep hillside, wherever one looked, one saw campfires smoking and glowing in the dusk. The smell of woodsmoke, the sound of axes in the thickets, the sight of men hauling wood, kindling it, piling it on, or, when the last daylight was gone, carrying fiery brands of it to light the way between one fire and the next, these were my first sensations as we rode among the army of the West Saxons encamped under Ashdown. Next after this I became aware of multitudes of horses, tethered in long rows, stamping, tossing up their heads, the whites of their eyes red with firelight, snorting because of the smoke.

At a crossing of two paths a troop of horsemen barred our way. They stood halted. Weapons glimmered in the glow. Their leader hailed us:

"Ho, there! We are Hampshire men newly arrived. Tell us where we can find the banners of our shire."

"You are right out of your way," Guntram replied. "Hampshire men lie yonder, back the way you have come, about half a mile. These are King's men."

"Not so neither, master," a bystander called out. "The King's men moved out of here this afternoon. They've gone back to new lines over toward Wantage."

Guntram cursed. "Stone of darkness, then we are all at odds together! Good night, Hampshire men. Remember that the common lot of all soldiering is looking for men in the dark in a strange country!"

We rode off again through more and more regions of campfires, till presently over the roof of a farmstead Guntram recognized a pennon embroidered with a red dragon. He led us into the yard and hailed several of the soldiers there by name, in a friendly fashion. To us he said:

"These are men of the King's bodyguard. You had best stay with them tonight, and I will come for you again in the morning." He briefly explained our business to one or two who were at hand, then rode off again into the smoky night. The soldiers found us shelter and some straw. They found hay for the pony and food for ourselves before settling down for the night. There was little talking. Indeed the whole camp, as I remember it, was very quiet except for the crackle of the fires, the snort and jingle of horses shaking their bridles, and, every now and then, the distant challenge of a sentry.

Guntram did not come the next morning, for, as we learned later, he could not find the place again—it turned out to lie a long way from the lord Alfred's quarters—and the events of that day gave him little time.

Three great things I saw that morning: the White Horse, the stone church and the King.

The first was spread out in gigantic whiteness on the hillside above the camp, a huge beast which had been cut bare in the chalk in ancient times, long before Noah's flood. The fringes of the Wessex camp reached up to it, and tiny figures, the soldiery of King Ethelred, moved like ants around its body.

The second, the stone church, was among some trees not far from us. We were told that it had been built under the instruction of the holy St. Birinus himself, during his mission into this part of Britain two hundred years before. It was the first stone building I had ever seen; and it was here that I saw the King Ethelred. He came in the morning sun, in procession with the banners of his army and of the saints and churches from all the country around, with a golden cross and with clouds of incense, preceded by the Bishops of Sherborne and Dorchester, and the monks of the monastery of Abingdon, and followed by the thanes of his household and the ealdormen of his shires, each with his followers. The ringing of bells and the singing of the monks filled all the air. The King himself was a

tall man, with fair hair and beard, but not handsome in the face although he was very well proportioned, majestic in his bearing, and splendidly dressed. He wore over his silken tunic a golden breastplate in the style of the emperors of old Rome, upon which were fashioned images of the twelve apostles, and Christ on the cross adored by angels. This breastplate, it was said, had been a gift from the Emperor Charlemagne to Egbert of Wessex, the King's grandfather. Egbert and his son Ethelwulf, and two of Ethelwulf's sons, who had been the elder brothers of this Ethelred, and kings of Wessex before him, all had worn this breastplate in their time.

But there was a look in the eyes of the King which I had seen before in another king's face. As he walked, his eyes were fixed with passionate zeal upon a jeweled coffer carried before him on the shoulders of four priests, and in this, I was told afterward, were the bones of many saints which had been sent to the King by the Pope himself. Around the King's neck, also, and upon the golden armlets which he wore, there hung a great number of little crosses, and medals and other holy emblems. I had seen this look, this devotion, these crosses before, in the eyes and upon the thin body of King Edmund of East Anglia, and to see it here again on the eve of another battle, in the eyes of another king, awaiting the same foe, made me for a moment afraid.

The King passed on amid the incense into the church, to pray for God's grace upon his army. Then he and the whole procession came out again and went through all the ranks of the army, stopping often to pray. They went up the hillside to the edges of the White Horse, from where, looking back over the plain, they could see yet more companies of men on horse and foot marching in to swell the army from distant parts of the kingdom. But from the other direction there came one horseman alone, spurring in a lather, capless, cloakless, spattered with flying mud, tiny over the ridge and along the bare brow of the Downs from the direction of Reading, shouting something as he passed unchecked through the outlying picket lines, then down the steep hillside, horse and all to the nearest ranks of the army shouting as he came: "To arms! The Danes are coming! Their whole army is on the march!"

The West Saxons had withdrawn to this place under Ashdown to gather their strength for another attack upon the stronghold at Reading; they had not expected the enemy to march out in this manner to meet them. Indeed it is not easy to say why the Danes had done so. Probably they thought to take the Christians by surprise before they had recovered from their first defeat, and thus to destroy them forever. But King Ethelred had posted spies with relays of horses along the hills to keep watch on Reading, and it was because of this that the news had been brought so swiftly. The distance to Reading over the hills was twenty-five miles, and it was unlikely that the heathen would come up in time to join battle that day; but it was expected for the following morning. The King did not return again to his hall in Wantage. He sent his trumpeter to summon forward his bodyguard of King's men. His tent was pitched in a fold of the hills, and above that, not far off, upon a green mound, he set up his battle standard, the Dragon of Wessex, side by side with the Standard of the Cross. The Christian troops marched forward under their shire leaders up the sides of Ashdown Hill. In long files or little groups, like dark dragons bristling with spears and winged with pennants, they wended up and over the white body of the ancient horse.

Down in the valley where only serfs and grooms remained to guard the baggage, the monk Esdras and I watched the last companies of King's men march off over the fields. Then came some on horseback with a banner, riding hard, and I recognized the lord Alfred, with his thanes, and Guntram among them. The Frankish knight saw us as he passed and wheeled aside from the others to speak to us.

"This battle comes sooner than we thought," he said, "and I have been unable to help you in so short a time. Seek me again later. You will find me somewhere hammering out the dints in my helmet, but by God's grace you will find me still alive. I have a skin and a skull like old King Charlemagne's elephant, so never fear for me. Farewell."

In the farmyard the monk Esdras kicked at an iron pot which stood abandoned beside the fire. His eyes were wide and glazed, for now the angel of bloodshed was dinning in his heart and even the noise of the cooking pot as it rolled from his foot sounded to him like the clash of helmets in battle. He strode restlessly up and down. Presently he took the two arrows of St.

Edmund and tied them together with a cord, crosswise. This cross he then secured to the top of a long pole. Then raising it high over his head he cried out:

"Woe to them, the killers and spillers of saint's blood! Evil come to the wicked ones, the burners, the spoilers, the spurners of churches! Under this cross of arrows, the sign of their guilt, let them melt, let them pour away spilt like filthy water!"

He looked at me, but I think that his eyes, burning bright with the ecstasy of his angel, did not see me. He strode out and away toward the place of battle, carrying the cross of arrows, leaving me alone.

Late in the afternoon the two armies came in sight of each other. The scouts on both sides posted ahead on horseback, and having measured high words with each other, galloped back to their own armies. The heathen halted for the night beyond a hill two miles away from the Christians.

Outside his tent King Ethelred held a war council. He said:

"The heathen have drawn up their army to fight, not in one host, as is usual, but in two. We learn that one of these hosts is led by the two kings Halfdan and Bagsec; the other by the vile Guthorm, and Sidroc, son of the jarl whom Ethelwulf slew, and many other jarls, too many to mention. Therefore we also will form up in two hosts. I, the King, will command the host of the right flank, against the two kings of the heathen. Alfred, my brother, will command the host of the left, against the host of their jarls."

This was received with approval. The King then went on to divide his army, and in the order he gave them, each lord and his men took their places for the night, ready to advance at dawn to the chosen battle place. Their horses they sent to safety in the rear, as was customary.

The night was cold, the stars shone brilliantly over the white frost. The armies slept around their clustered fires. The King slept little and rose before dawn to pray. The lord Alfred came armed to his tent and found him on his knees.

"Kneel here with me, brother," said the King, "for we will need the strong arm of God's grace with us today as never before. I have sent for the priest, so that we may say Mass together before we go out."

"Your are right, brother," said Alfred. "But we must make haste, even with our prayers, for the stars are growing pale already. Morning is at hand and the army is waiting for you to lead them to the battle place. Look, even your banners are eager to advance." He pointed to the two dark shapes of the banners, the Cross and the Dragon, where they flapped in the dawn wind against the gray sky.

"The Mass may not be taken in haste, brother," said the King, "and we of all people, being answerable for the fate of so great an army, dare not go into battle without the Sacrament. Neither may we go unshriven."

The King's Mass priest came to the tent shortly after and the two brothers knelt to confess their sins. Outside upon the green mound, the banners flapped and shook their poles. A man came running. Battle thanes, helmeted, carrying great shields, came running. The sentries at the King's tent barred the way.

"Let me pass," cried a voice. "I am Alfgar of Dorset. I have news for the King."

They let him pass and he came quickly into the tent. The King did not move from his knees, nor did he even look around to see who entered.

"Under the mercy of God, but I must speak," said Alfgar. "King, the heathen are already beginning to march from their camp."

The King hesitated for a second, then finished his prayer with the priest, crossed himself, and rose to his feet.

"Is this certain?" he asked. "It is not yet light."

"They mean to fall upon us before we are in the field," said Alfgar. "But they reckon us too easy a prey. We stand ready to advance. Come now, lord King, and advance your banners."

The King replied, "Alfgar, I must do God's service first. After I have said Mass I will come to lead them up."

Anxiety was in the face of Ealdorman Alfgar. Outside, other voices were calling. "Lead us to the field, lord King! Advance the banners!"

The King knelt again, and the priest continued to say the Mass. The lord Alfred, kneeling, looked over his shoulder and saw gray dawn in the doorway. Alfgar the Ealdorman stood yet in the tent, and in the entrance others waited. Outside the whole army waited, while the banners tugged and flapped on the green mound.

"Brother," said Alfred softly to the King, "you are right in what you do; but one of us two must go. I will go, and lead the army into the field and hold the line until you come. Pray for me also, but come soon."

Then the lord Alfred rose up and went out, helmeted. The armed lords stood at his back. The horn sounded and the banners were lifted. They went forward up the green hill; and the long ranks of the host to the right and left of them moved forward darkly in the growing light toward the battle place. Only the King's bodyguard remained waiting, drawn up near the tent. They could hear the heathen advancing from the distance, their horn calls carried before them on the wind.

8

Three at Ashdown

I. GUNTRAM

THE ARMY marched now on foot. Only the commanders and a few of their chief thanes were mounted.

I, Guntram, rode on the left side of my lord Alfred. On his right he had his trumpeter. Behind him came the standard-bearers and a strong guard of his thanes. Farther back, to right and left of us in two great divisions marched the army of the West Saxons, like two great forests moving.

Our march led us up to the top of Ashdown near a place where it is crested with a long grassy bank which, it is said, men had dug for a rampart in ancient times. Not far below this crest, on the hillside, there was an old thorn tree, twisted and wind-bitten. The sky grew red with dawn; and at the same time there appeared upon the crest of the hill in front of us a long wall of armed men. They were the heathen. My lord Alfred halted and bade his trumpeter sound. All the horns and trumpets sounded to halt, the banners came to the front and the shield-wall was formed along the length of the Saxon army. The shield-wall of the pagans stood fast along the ridge.

The lord Alfred looked at me with a wry smile. "What do you say to this, Guntram?" he asked.

"Only that the devil is in it," said I. "They've beaten us to the high ground. We should have marched sooner."

"Ay, and now we shall have to sweat for it, King's brother," said a man who was standing near. Britnoth his name was. He was an old fighter, full of scars.

"It that you, Britnoth?" said my lord Alfred. "But you have known worse and come well out of it."

"Ay, I have," said Britnoth, "but see you, King's brother, the worst of this place is not the hill, but the sun. We shall have to fight with it dazzling in our eyes."

Alfgar of Dorset, Ethelnoth of Somerset, and other ealdormen and lords of the shires now came riding to the lord Alfred. Those from the right wing, which the King himself was to lead into battle, said anxiously:

"Lord Alfred, our men will not keep their spirits up for long in this bad place. Will the King come soon?"

"Soon," said Alfred. "Stand firm. We will wait."

"Lord, we cannot wait," said Alfgar. "If the heathen

attack now they can come down with all their weight upon us, with the hill and the sun in their favor. It might go ill with us. Better that we should go forward and break their rush halfway."

Ethelnoth of Somerset said, "That is true. Lead us up now, lord Alfred. All will follow you."

Alfred answered, "Such a thing is against all the custom of war. The power to give the order for battle belongs to the King alone. Not even I, his brother, may take that power upon myself without very great reason. That our King is now on his knees seeking God's help to give us victory this day—is that reason enough, do you think?"

They answered ruefully, "No, it is not enough. We must wait, then."

Alfred said, "Yes, we must wait. But there is also some advantage in it. The sun, which at present dazzles in our eyes, will not last long. See how those clouds are coming up. It will not be a bad thing to wait till they have covered the sun."

This also we saw was true, and the leaders returned to their own men, to hold them steady till the King came.

"Yet it is hard to stand here and listen to the heathen dogs snarling and jeering at us," growled Britnoth.

"None the less you must bite your shield and hold your tongue, old leatherface," said Alfred. "It will not be for long."

Then Alfred rode up and down in front of the army, calling on the men to stand firm till the King came. At the same time there came riding out from the heathen array a number of their jarls, at full gallop on horseback. There was one, a young gallant on a gray horse who made a great show of his horsemanship, racing and reining in and rearing up, and shaking his ax toward our ranks. Shouts of rage were heard among the Saxons.

"Come up, then!" shouted the vikings. "Come up the hill, ye dung-carriers! We are ready to make hay with ye! Come up!"

"See how they stand quaking!" shouted others. "Milk-cheeks! Tremble-knees! Come up the hill and we'll roll ye down again!"

The young man on the gray horse was a famous fighter. His name was Harald. His horse now bolted forward suddenly. He curbed it and it reared up high.

"See, ye Saxons, this is a Saxon horse, the brute! See how I master it! See how I give it the spur!" He jagged the spur. The horse bolted fast along the hill. He reined it in hard, and again it reared up. Then as once more it began to bolt forward under his spur, it stumbled and with a swerve fell, and threw the viking sprawling in the grass. From the Saxons there went up a roar of laughter.

"Dogs!" cried Harald the jarl. "See what I do!"

He lifted his ax and slew the horse with one blow, splitting its skull. None the less the Saxons did not stop laughing.

"Stand fast, all men," cried Alfred still, as he went down the line. We dismounted now and sent our horses back to be with the others and stood with our shields ready for battle. The heathen jarls too went back into their host.

"Now it is coming, Guntram," said the lord Alfred to me in a low voice. "But is the King coming? I do not wish the men to see me looking back. Do you look."

I looked back and said, "Not yet, lord."

Then the lord Alfred said to me, "Guntram, you have known me a long while. I think you have not ever had reason to think me a coward."

I answered, "Never, lord. But this is the moment before battle when all men fear a little what is to come. Even I. Even old Britnoth there, biting his shield."

"But I fear something more than that," said Alfred. "All my life I have feared the moment when I might have to stand alone in the King's place. Each of my brothers has worn the crown of Wessex; but I, being the youngest, had cause to hope that this, and what it stands for, would not come my way. Oh, do not mistake me; the power and wealth that belong to the highborn, all that I like well enough; but I have always hoped to spend my life in a different way. Not in the way of a king. Certainly not like this, as a leader in battle."

"None the less, you have the knack of it," said I, and that was the truth.

"It is a knack that belongs to my kindred," he replied, "and I have to do what I can."

Hardly had he said this when there came a shout from the ranks on all sides:

"Arrows! Arrows! Shields up!"

A cloud of arrows rose up from the heathen army on

the ridge, and came flighting down toward us with a hiss. They thudded and stuck in shield and grass, but though the line swayed under the hail I saw no one hurt.

Alfred then looked around. He saw the Wessex men standing fast on the slope, but he did not see the King coming.

"Shields up! Arrows!" cried voices again. The sun dazzled in our faces. The arrows hissed down.

"King's brother," cried old Britnoth. "Lead us up! Must we stand here and be spitted for nothing? It is useless to wait longer. They will attack, if we do not."

"You are right, Britnoth," said Alfred. "Listen to me. If the King has not come by the time the sun goes into those clouds yonder, and so out of our eyes, I will wait no longer, but lead you up."

"Shields up!" cried Britnoth. The arrows thudded.

"Come up, ye dog-born Saxons!" mocked the heathen. "Come up, ye Christians, ye wet-legged ones!"

The cloud's edge crept toward the sun.

"Pass the word along," said Alfred. "Bowmen, be ready. My trumpeter, be ready to sound."

The King was not seen. We waited. The heathen jeered. Then the sun-dazzle suddenly went out, and for a moment all seemed darkly gray as the clouds closed in.

"Now!" cried the lord Alfred. "In the name of Christ, and in the name of the King!"

The trumpet sounded. The Saxon arrows flew among the heathen, and the Christian host went forward at a walking pace up the hill, shouting as they went. The heathen shouted in return, and came down to meet us. The armies met together with a great clash where the thorn tree grew on the hillside.

2. ESDRAS

... And the red birds and the birds of blackness flooded the sky with feathers of their blood till the sun itself was covered up; and the terrible tongues of battle, the high howl of the trumpets, the lean wolves baying, the stones crying out for pity and for hatred under the torn grass and the trampled iron, this terrible tumult from the hill reached the ears of the King praying in his tent.

I, Esdras the monk, stood outside the King's tent among the soldiers. I heard King Ethelred call out from the tent, "What is this noise I hear?" And the soldiers answered, "It is the noise of war, lord King. They have already joined battle on the hill."

Then the King called, "My armor!" They took his armor to the tent where he knelt for the blessing of God. Bishop Heahmund blessed the armor. The Bishop was himself armed for the battle; he was a mighty soldier. Then the King came out from his tent. He stood like a giant in his mail. His eyes shone like torches under the shadow of his helmet. Upon the helmet his crest was a golden boar, bristled for fighting. The King was armed with a great ax, and upon his shield and breastplate were many crosses of brass. When he came out, ready for battle, I called to him:

"King Ethelred, I bring you another cross to go with you into battle. Behold, the sharp cross of King Edmund, the arrows of the martyr!" And I held my cross high for him to see.

Heahmund the Bishop knew me, for I had been with him that night. He spoke now to the King, who turned and gazed with awe upon the cross.

"It is a sign, lord King," said the Bishop. *"In hoc signo vinces!"*

"So be it!" cried the King. "Monk, come with me! Carry the cross by my side!"

Like the crushing of millstones, the bone-fronted thrusting of savage bulls, like the flooded sea smiting and breaking against the walls of land, so the ranks of battle gripped and sweated on the hillside as the King drew near. A shout went up! "It is the King!" The horns blew. "It is the King!" The arrows flocked, and the red birds and the birds of blackness flew this way and that, and King Ethelred, like a cold sword plunged into the fire, seared a black way through the red ranks, swinging his ax. The heathen drew back, the Christians pressed shouting up the hill where the great king trod like a giant swinging his ax, farther and farther forward up the torn black earth of the mound to the top of all. The heathen drew back and the Christians gained the summit of the hill and stood ranked against the red birds and birds of blackness, and the two hosts stood panting and saying nothing, ready to begin the next onslaught. The ground between them was all spiked with spent arrows, thick as stubble. . . .

3. THE YOUNG ALFRED

I was left alone; yet I did not grieve to be parted from Esdras. His mood of bloodshed frightened me. He went up to the battle not so much like a man as like a hungry dog hunting. I remained below and watched the last of the army march away toward Ashdown Ridge. Then, not knowing what better to do, I harnessed the old pony and rode over to a village nearby to get food and shelter. While the armies were gathering on the hill, the serfs and laborers alone remained down here in the valley and went about their ordinary work as though nothing were afoot which could change their lives. And indeed for some of them one master, whether Saxon or Dane, was very like another; for in this part of the country there remained many communities of the old British or Welsh people, whose ancestors had been made slaves by the Saxons, and felt no loyalty to them in their hearts. They were ragged, dirty people. The Church cared for their souls and their masters cared for their labor, but they themselves cared only to avoid the Evil Ones and to enjoy the warmth of rubbing shoulders with their neighbors. In the dusk they sat outside their hut doors with their thick food-bowls in their laps and watched the now distant campfires twinkling in a long string away on the ridge. They had little to say about it all.

Among these poor folk I found shelter for the night. The floor of the hut where we slept was all composed of bones and ashes and filth, which had been trodden deep and hard underfoot for generations past.

Just before dawn the cold misty air of the valley stole into the hut and wakened me. I sat up in the dirty straw, shivering and listening. The noise I heard, though it was distant, and which at first I had mistaken for cattle lowing somewhere away in the mist, was the noise of the war horns on the hill. I went outside, but it was still too dark to see anything upon Ashdown, and as the light increased, so too did the valley mist. Through this, presently, a red sun began to glow, without warmth; and against the sunrise came long black flights of rooks filling the air with their hateful cries so that one could no longer hear those faint sounds from the hill.

The mist did not clear till later in the morning, and then at last we from the valley were able to see the ridge of Ashdown. All along its skyline and combed out down its sides were dark straggled shapes which we knew were ranks of men fighting. These shapes seemed hardly to move, except for a sort of writhing and glittering that went on within them, like bubbles rising in a cauldron. Once, though, as we watched, the whole mass shook out into two parts with a clear space between, and so it remained for what seemed a long while, unmoving. Then with a bulging movement toward each other, the two halves joined together again, the join closing the rift all the way along till there remained only the one dark mass. This seemed to be moving very slowly, with long hesitations, toward the east.

"The Danes!" someone shouted. "The Danes are going back!"

Suddenly there was a great movement in the armies.

Those on the eastward side of the mass of men were going back fast. Then the mass frayed out into groups of running men.

"The Danes! The Danes have broken!" came the shout again. And then: "Come on! Come on to the hill!"

All along Ashdown now I saw men running and fighting, running eastward, leaving behind them scattered clusters of fallen. Could it be possible that those running, those dead and those defeated men were the terrible heathen who had never in living memory been driven thus from the field? The evening before, as I had watched the Christian army go up to the place of battle, I had in my heart expected only the same sad end that I had known before: the scattering of my friends while the heathen army looted and burned all the land around, while I made my way to some new hiding place, or even came at last to learn that I was a slave in a land where there was no longer a Christian God. But here on the hill at Ashdown I now saw the pagans running and the Christians pursuing them till there were none but the dead in sight.

The villagers around me, men and women alike, were arming themselves with spades and axes and sticks, whatever came to hand, and going off toward the hill. I thought at first they were going to help in the pursuit of the enemy; but they were not. They were going up to plunder the dead and dying. A time like this might never come again—swords, rings, brooches, cloaks, all to be had for the taking, if folk were quick enough.

"Come along with your old pony, boy," said some of them to me. "We will lead you." Perhaps they thought they could use the pony later to help carry their plunder, and perhaps I would not have cared. But so as not to be left alone, and because I myself wanted to have some part in the victory, I willingly went with them. But the pony was not so willing and when we had got a little way up the hill it would not go any farther. The villagers tried to coax it, but it made slow going, and since this would have held them back they soon left me and my pony and hurried on up the hill and out of sight. As for me, I was not such a rider that I could take my mount where it did not wish to go, and as I could not go without him I had to go where he would take me. We thus went along the flank of the hill a little way, with no one in sight, until we came to a hollow in which there were some clumps of bushes. The pony made his way toward these, and as we passed among them a sound from behind me made me turn quickly and I saw a man rushing out at me, holding a broken spear. I knew at once that he was a Dane.

"Quick, boy, give me horse," he said. "Give horse, or thou a dead boy." At the same time he thrust at me with his broken spear to push me off. The pony swerved from him, turning around. To steady myself against this sudden movement and to protect myself from the thrust, I grabbed and held onto the spear with one hand, and to the pony's mane with the other. The man at the same time cried, "Ah, will ye! Then off!" and he made a grab to snatch my leg from the stirrup, meaning to pitch me headlong. But by chance the pony in turning had brought my right side toward him, and there was no leg there for him to seize. In the moment of his astonishment he lost his balance. At the same time I thrust at him with his own spear, and the pony gave another lurch. The Dane stumbled and fell. I found myself with the great spear in one hand, pulling at the reins with the other to prevent the pony throwing me also. At the same time I heard a cry from the man on the ground behind me. As soon as the pony was still, I looked back and saw him still lying there, but trying with many groans to rise. It seemed he could not.

"Thy beast, thy cursed beast hath trod on me," he moaned. "I think it hath broke my leg. Help me up."

I did not trust him. I was afraid of cunning. I answered, "Not I. Little help you would have given me if you'd had your way."

"By the hammer!" he swore. "I would not have hurt thee! Thou art a devil, thou with thy one leg! Oh, my leg! Thou hast killed me, boy. Or now the Saxons will kill me, even if thou dost not thyself. Look, boy, I not hurt thee. Help me up and sell me thy horse. I pay money!" He put his hand in the neck of his tunic and brought out a little bag hanging on a string around his neck. He held it up to me. "Come thou, and get," he said.

I shook my head.

"Come get. I pay," he repeated, but I was afraid to go near him.

At this moment some of the village people came

around the hillside. They ran toward us shouting, "Here's one! Quick, get hold of him! Kill him!"

The Dane tried once more to rise, then, almost fainting, sank back and said, "Finish. Finish." He closed his eyes and became quite calm. The villagers ran up brandishing their spades. At the sight of them I felt a sudden pity for the man. I called out to the villagers:

"This man is mine. Stand away!"

"Yours, is he?" said one of the village men. "Get away from him, boy, or we'll split you open before we do the same to him."

I was afraid of them all, but I could not bear to see them kill the man before my eyes—to see them strike, to see him bleed and cease to move.

"Let him alone!" I cried. "He is mine for blood-money! Stand back!" I made as if to go for them with the spear I held, but the old pony stood stock-still, and one of the men wrenched the spear out of my hand and laughed at me. I was helpless.

"I have friends near at hand on the hill," I cried. I hardly expected to be believed, but none the less in a desperate attempt to make it seem true I shouted at the top of my voice, "Help! Help!"

To my astonishment I was answered.

"Hola there," came a voice from the hillside. "What's amiss?"

I turned and saw at a little distance the big and friendly figure of Guntram the Frank.

"Help, Guntram, help!" I cried. He was on horseback. He had with him a spare horse and a groom.

Leaving these where they were, he dismounted and came on foot down the hill. Seeing him so stark in his huge Frankish armor the villagers drew back.

"What's amiss here?" said Guntram, at my side. I explained, breathlessly. The Dane had propped himself on one elbow and was watching us.

When I had finished, Guntram turned toward the villagers, who were now standing at a little distance. Some, indeed, had gone away altogether. The rest, except for the man who had taken the spear from me, were about to follow.

"You," said Guntram to this man, "do you not wish to go also?"

"I meant no wrong, lord," replied the man. "Only to cut off the head of this heathen dog. You would do the same."

"Very likely," said Guntram. He turned to the Dane. "And why should he not cut off your head, my viking, hey?"

"I belong to the boy," said the Dane. "I will pay the boy my blood-price."

"And why should the boy not slay you himself and take your money also?" demanded Guntram.

"He will if he will," said the Dane.

Guntram looked at me. I shook my head. The Dane saw it and said, "He will not. I give thanks to Odin the Wise."

"Heathen!" exclaimed Guntram. "For saying that I could kill you here and now, I myself, with my own red hand. See my sword. Odin is not wise. Thor is not strong. All your gods are deaf and weak and cannot lift a finger to help you. Cast them away. Christ is stronger. You shall be baptized a Christian. If you vow to do this your life shall be spared. If not—"

The man lay in silence for a minute, groaning and feeling his leg. At last he said with a sigh, "I will. I swear it. Help me up. I will be baptized. Oh, my leg! Oh, how the gods have deserted me!"

Guntram said, "That is well, and very wise of you, viking." He called out to the village man who was still standing near. "You! Come here and listen to me. I am Guntram, the lord Alfred's man, and if you disobey me I will see to it that you are skinned alive and hung up for the crows to eat. Do you understand?"

The man said, "Yes, lord. I will not disobey."

"Do you know Wiglaf the Reeve?"

"Yes, lord. He is the lord Alfred's reeve at Wantage."

"You are right," said Guntram. "Now take this boy and this heathen man to Wiglaf the Reeve and tell him that I have sent them. If you fail to take them there safely, I will have you cut all into little pieces three fingers wide."

"Yes, lord, I understand, lord," said the man, pulling his forelock.

"And you, boy, stay there at the lord Alfred's house, in the care of Wiglaf, till I come for you. See to it that this heathen goes to the priest to be baptized as he has promised, and tell them at Wantage that the King and the lord Alfred will sleep this night like conquerors in Reading town. Farewell!"

He turned to go up the hill. Only then did I remember the great thing that had happened that day.

"Guntram!" I called after him. "What news of the battle?"

"It is over," he shouted back. "A great victory! The heathen are finished and we are scattering them like chaff in the wind. The whole of Ashdown is full of their corpses. Their king, Bagsec, lies dead. Their jarls, Harald and Osbiorn and Sidroc, all lie dead. Halfdan runs before us like a rabbit, Guthorm bolts like a hare. We shall have them all in the pot before nightfall!"

My prisoner groaned again. "O gods!" I heard him mutter. "O hidden and departed ones!"

9

The Dane-Leg

W<small>IGLAF THE REEVE</small> took me into the household of the lord Alfred at Wantage. Here also the heathen Dane had his leg put in a splint, and as soon as he was fit to hobble about he was baptized by the Mass priest. I saw little more of him, and never had a blood-price for him, for after I had lived two months at Wantage bad fortune came again. All the Wessex people were driven out, and the royal lands and houses of the King and the lord Alfred were left to be plundered by the heathen. So then this Dane spat upon Christ and rejoined his own people.

But I kept the broken spear I had taken from him on Ashdown, and with it I became Dane-Leg. It happened in this way: There was at Wantage a famous smith named Pedda, and one day soon after I came there, while the victory was still with us, I took him my spear and asked him to mount the blade on a new shaft for me.

"And what will you do with it?" he asked, laughing. "Would you be a fighting man, you with your one leg?"

I was hurt and angry at being mocked.

"I have taken a battle prisoner already, and captured his weapon from his hand," I answered. "Have I not the right to carry the spear?"

"It is true," replied Pedda, and he took off the iron spear blade from the shaft. But then, instead of throwing the broken shaft aside, he stood for a moment looking at it. It was of stout ash wood. He came and measured the length of it against my leg.

It was the same almost to an inch.

"Here, now, is a better thing than a spear for you," said Pedda. "You shall have your captured spear, but you shall also have a captured leg into the bargain—a leg seized in battle from your enemy; an ash-leg from Ashdown; a Dane-leg from the Dane!"

I thought at first he was mocking me again; but he was in earnest.

"Look," he said, "I will forge an iron harness on this spear shaft, so that it can be strapped onto the stump of your leg. And I will put an iron ferrule at the other end, and as you put it to the ground you can say: 'Thus do I, Alfred the One-Legged, make my enemy serve my turn!'"

He was as good as his word. The Dane-leg was made in a few days and fitted to me, and I stood on it for the first time in the forge of Pedda the Smith while Wiglaf himself and a crowd of the lord Alfred's house people watched me. I stood unsteadily.

"Make a step, now," said Pedda. "One step."

I balanced on my own leg and planted the Dane-leg a pace forward. Then with a clumsy movement I jerked my leg up level with it. The harness hurt me, but I tried again, and this time I managed to swing my leg ahead of the stump. Wiglaf and his people clapped their hands and encouraged me, and I took another pace. But this time I stumbled and fell. Pedda, who was behind, caught me and stood me up again, but the harness had bruised me badly, and it hurt me to go on. Pedda gave me my new spear, and with this to support me I stumped on to the doorway and with the friendly crowd all around me, made my way out into the open courtyard before the hall. As I labored clumsily along, partly hopping, partly leaning on my spear, and every now and then trying my whole weight upon the stump, and with all the people going along with me, laughing and encouraging me and putting out hands to help me whenever it looked as if I might fall, the lord Alfred rode into the courtyard on the far side, with a number of his thanes. No one noticed him until he had dismounted and come over with Guntram to see what was happening. Then the crowd drew back respectfully to let him through. But I, sweating and out of breath, with the Dane-leg hurting my bruised thigh, stood resting, my head down, leaning my weight on my spear, and I did not see who was standing there until the lord Alfred himself spoke to me. "I wish to see the leg. Stay as you are," he said, and then he knelt, and handed me the skirt of my tunic, bidding me hitch it up out of the way, while he carefully examined the Dane-leg and its harness. Pedda came out of the crowd which had made a ring around us, and knelt beside the lord Alfred, saying, "I made it, lord. It can be made easier for him, here and here. He should have a leather sleeve around his stump, and a padding of lamb's wool where the weight comes." They bade me walk a little again, watching the action as I went. Then the lord Alfred himself unfastened the straps and took off the Dane-leg and examined my leg.

"Guntram has told me of you," he said. "You are the boy who came with the monk from East Anglia, are you not? The monk is with the King now. I saw him at Ashdown. Have they told you about him?"

I said, "No, lord."

"He went into the battle bare-sark, stark naked," said he. "He stood in front of the shield-wall and tore off his robe, and no weapon touched him. He stood at the King's side, carrying the arrow-cross of Edmund with both hands above his head cursing the pagans by the holy name of God. And he went forward treading in their blood. He was sent to us from God, that is certain."

Then having again examined my leg, he asked when it had been done, and by whom. I answered as always, that I did not know, that it had been done long ago in my childhood. For I no longer thought of myself as a child, child though I still was.

"This too is a miracle," said Alfred. "How is it possible to take off a child's limb, and still mend his body? And you came here with the monk . . ." After a slight pause he went on. "Guntram tells me that you are called by my name."

I answered, "Yes, lord."

"And that you have come with some message or some gift for me?"

I answered, "With both, lord." But my conscience smote me. The old bridle lay under my pillow, but it was a long time since I had dreamed of it, and the dream had grown thin. I feared I should no longer know how to give the thing to Alfred, or what to say.

But at that time I did not have to say anything more, for the circle of the crowd opened again and Guntram said to Alfred, "Lord, the lady Elswitha is here."

The lord Alfred turned and greeted his wife, kissing her on both cheeks. She had come from the women's bower, with several of her waiting women who knelt to Alfred while the lady Elswitha handed him the drink of welcome in a silver cup. She was a small woman with gray eyes and dark hair which one could see as a shadow through the finely woven blue veil she wore around her head and shoulders, fastened with a brooch of gold from Byzantium.

As they turned to go toward the hall the lord Alfred said to me, "Bring me your gift in the hall this evening, after supper."

When he had gone I went to my bedplace at the back of Pedda's smithy, and while he was busy altering the Dane-leg I took out the bridle from under my pillow and thought how to make it look worthy to be given to a king's brother. I rubbed it with fat and tallow to make it softer, and I polished the old buckles, unstiffening them. It was better, but still I was ashamed of it. I hid it under my cloak when I went into the hall that evening. I sat among the household people and watched the lord Alfred in his high place in the center. It was a dark night, but within the hall there was torchlight and firelight, and singing when the mead was poured out. Alfred sat silent, and listened to his thanes boasting the deeds they had done at Ashdown, and would do again in the next battle with the heathen. As I sat watching him he looked across and saw me, and beckoned me over to him, and he spoke to his neighbor, a gray-haired man, who turned and watched me as I crossed the hall. There was now a minstrel singing near the high table, and all were silent listening to him. The lord Alfred made a sign to me to sit on a stool nearby. The minstrel was singing of Egbert the Great, grandfather of the lord Alfred, and of his deeds at the court of the Emperor Charlemagne; how he fought against the Moorish and Bohemian pagans with the Emperor's paladins before he came home to claim his kingdom in Wessex; and how he then marched against the Mercians and subdued them, and made them acknowledge him as High King of all the English south of Humber. Beneath my cloak with my fingers I felt the harness. I had found it in Mercia. I remembered the Mercian monk Oswy who had smiled and winked at the news of the Danish march on Wessex. He had said that the royal house of Wessex was under a curse. "Of the four grandsons of Egbert two have already died wearing the crown. The third is Ethelred who wears it today. And when the Danes have finished with him there will remain only the last, the youngest brother, a poor creature cursed with an incurable sickness, who is taken up with piety and book reading."

The minstrel plucked at the harpstrings. The lord Alfred sat without eating, listening thoughtfully. Incurable sickness? Were his cheeks pale? The smoke-light flittered about his face. The minstrel ended his song, proclaiming the heroic future of Egbert's house, and the thanes banged the long tables with their fists, applauding him. He stood up and Alfred handed him the mead cup.

When the minstrel had gone Alfred turned to me and said, "Now for the young Dane-Leg! Have you brought me the thing you have to give?"

I answered, "Yes, lord," and put my hand upon it under my cloak. But I felt the spirit was no longer in it. My hand felt the old straps that the grease had not well softened, and my mind could not reach the message I ought to give. Was there no longer a voice within to guide me? If there was, it was only the one which said: "The time is wrong."

Nevertheless I took the harness from under my cloak and pushed it slowly forward upon the table before the lord Alfred and the gray-haired man who sat by him, and the thanes on each side. It upset the ale horn, the ale spilling all over the table. The lord Alfred put his hand upon the harness and waited for me to speak, but my mind was empty. I could only think that this was the wrong time. At last my tongue spoke for me, saying only:

"Lord Alfred, this is what I had to bring."

Alfred asked, "Had you no message to bring with it?"

I answered, "No, lord, but I had to bring this. I was told to give it to my namesake."

Some of the thanes laughed. But Alfred, unsmiling, asked, "But to me? Are you sure of this? Am I your only namesake? Can you remember nothing else?"

I said, "I cannot remember. It has left me. I am ashamed, lord Alfred. It has left me."

I stood holding onto the table, fighting against tears. I turned miserably to go. But as I did so the lord Alfred said:

"Alfred, young Dane-Leg, be patient. It is the time, not you, that is wrong."

I turned again and saw in his face that he believed in me, more than I had at that time believed in myself. I could not speak. The tears flowed down my cheeks. I brushed them away with my cloak.

"Sit down again," said Alfred, "and listen to me. The time will come. Whatever it is that has left you will come back. You must wait. Take back your gift now, and when the right time comes you will know it. Then, wherever I may be or whatever the hour, you must bring it to me. Let that be known between us."

I nodded, still unable to speak, and he went on. "So while we wait for the time you must stay with my household. And since you are here I have work for you."

He paused. I waited.

"Is it true," he asked, "that you were brought up by the monks in East Anglia?" And when I said it was true he went on. "Tell me, did they teach you to read and write?"

Remembering old Githo I answered, "There was one who I think could read, lord, and I think he meant to teach me. But he never did so."

"Would you learn now?" asked Alfred.

I answered with much hesitation, "Highborn, I want to learn how to be like other men when I am a man. I want to learn to be the master of my misfortune, to ride, and to fight with sword and shield. I do not want to learn to be different from other men, to read and write and sit apart."

But the lord Alfred replied:

"You are different. You will always be different. Do not waste your strength trying to fight battles that are already lost. You cannot win other men's battles or fight with their weapons. You are different, your weapons are yours alone, and your battle is new. Look," he said, motioning with his hand up and down the table where the thanes sat at supper, "look at all these stark heroes of mine. Look at their hands."

The smokelight flitted about their hands, clenched, meat-seizing, cup-holding, opening and closing, sinewy, thick-fingered, knobbed and knuckled, horny-nailed and butcher-scarred.

"They are the hands of brave fighting men," said Alfred, "who have to hold the wall of God's land against the strong flood of the heathen. But who will remember the blows they gave or the deeds they did, when the breath is out of their bodies? Their grandchildren's children may not even remember their names. Only the pen and the ink remembers, and only the reading eye can hear the voice of the pen. But which of these big jointy fingers can curl itself around a pen, even to write its own name? Speak, you Britnoth; can you hold a pen?"

"Ha, ha!" croaked old Britnoth with a rook's mirth, and held out his oak-tree hands with two fingers missing. "Hammers and axes are the best pens for my grip."

"But this boy's hands are young," said Alfred, "and if he is taught to use a pen as well as you can use an ax, you, and all like you, and all your deeds will rest in his hands from the day you die until Doomsday. Even there in the High Court of Heaven it needs an angel with a book and a pen to record our names and deeds, good or ill. Yet here on earth in my brother's kingdom, and over the whole of this land of England and over all of Europe north of Rome City, Christ's mankind lies beaten down in the path of this lusty tribe of ignorant heathen men, not half so much because our highborn men cannot stand and fight, as because they cannot read or write. The watchfires of all our futures are going out because we think it is enough to have kept our own selves warm in the few remaining embers of our past. . . . Do you understand me, Britnoth?"

"Not quite, lord," said Britnoth, "but I always like to hear you say things I cannot quite understand, so long as I can believe there's some sense in them. Meanwhile I understand that you mean to have this boy taught to read and write, and there's sense in that, right enough."

He turned then to me and said, "Boy, you came here with your gift for Alfred, and what the worth of that may be I do not know. But I know the worth of the gift he is offering you in return. I have seen the lord Alfred himself in his tent on the battlefield teaching himself his letters out of a book. By Christ's Cross, I would that God had made me as one-legged as yourself if at your age I could have been offered such a gift as this by such a man as my lord Alfred. Look in my eye, boy! I am not joking."

I said, "I will do as the lord Alfred commands."

"No," said Alfred, "it is not a command, but a free gift I offer you, as Britnoth says. You are free to refuse it now; but here is your teacher, if you accept."

He pointed to the gray-haired man at his side, who had been studying me without any expression throughout all of this. He was the monk John the Lombard, a faithful friend to Alfred, as was shown in time. Alfred had many other scholars in days to come, and many more learned than John the Lombard; but it was this man who went along with him among the battlefields of these hard times, and it was this man who taught me to read and write, not without difficulty.

"Yes, lord," I said to Alfred. "I accept. I will do truly what you expect of me."

"That is good," said he, and rose then from the table and went out, John the Lombard following. It was the time he kept for his prayers. The bridle he had left lying on the table. I picked it up and put it again under my cloak and left the hall. I was perplexed. I had failed in one task, and had been given another which, truth to tell, I did not want to do.

The next day a messenger came from the King, and Alfred and his thanes departed in haste to join him. A few days later the Saxon army faced the heathen again at the place called Basing. They fought a hard battle, but in the end the heathen had the victory. The Saxons were driven in all directions, and were glad of the nightfall to cover their retreat.

10

The King at Easter

KING ETHELRED set up his standard at Winchester and once more gathered his army together. He knew that the pagans had suffered heavily, although they had held the field, and he judged that by striking soon he could destroy them. They had withdrawn again to their stronghold at Reading, but King Ethelred, like a boar in the long grass, lay in wait for any that ventured out of the camp. Therefore they dared not venture in small numbers, and the West Saxons waited eagerly for them to come with all their remaining strength. But then bad news came. King Ethelred's spies from the woods above Reading reported that a great new army from Denmark had sailed up the Thames in their long ships, and had reinforced the pagans, who were now as strong as ever before, if not

stronger. So now the King was obliged to wait again while he gathered further strength for his own army, and had to watch the hungry pagans ravaging like a swarm of devils ever farther and farther afield in search of food and plunder. They laid waste the countryside for two months before the West Saxons were again strong enough to march against them. Then they met at the place called Marten, which lies about twenty miles north of Winchester, beside the Roman road. The Saxons fought as never before, until the pagans lay dying everywhere in the woods and ditches where they had crawled for shelter. None the less, because of their great numbers the pagans once again had the victory. Heahmund, Bishop of Sherborne, was killed in that battle, and King Ethelred himself was carried away wounded, wrapped in his cloak. They brought him back in blood and weakness to Winchester, where he rested several days.

During all this time I had stayed at Wantage with the lord Alfred's people, but now all the regions north of the Wiltshire plain were unsafe for us, and, two days after the battle of Marten, Guntram the Frank came, with as many horsemen as could be spared for an escort, to bid us pack up all we could and follow him south. The lord Alfred was at Badbury, near Wimborne, where, while the King was recovering from his wound, he was gathering the Saxon forces to defend all the southern and central parts of Wessex, since for the time being he could no longer hold the north. We set out from Wantage with heavy hearts. The lady Elswitha herself was with us, Alfred's wife, with their two-year-old daughter and their baby son of nine months. They rode in a wagon, meanly dressed and under a canopy of drab cloth so as to attract no attention to our journey. Our train of wagons and baggage animals made a sad sight wending over the Down under the windy March sky. I looked about me, half expecting still to find some fragments of Ashdown battle as we crossed the ridge, a victory only two months old, but now so far away. Sigeric, the Ealdorman of Berkshire, Ethelwulf's successor, joined us with some of his men during the most dangerous part of our journey; then he left us to return again to the north, to defend his land. Wiglaf the Reeve, with Pedda the Smith and many others who had befriended me at Wantage, remained behind with Sigeric to keep the royal estates so long as they could. Only I, with John the Lombard, my teacher, were sent for with the women and children. But I rode the pony, alongside Guntram in his great pot-helmet, who as we went told me of his ancestor Guntram Boso the Wicked, and of how he aspired to love the fierce Brunhild, Queen of the Franks, and of her wars with Queen Fredegond, and how they and their terrible husbands the sons of Lothaire ruined the whole land of France between them; and how Guntram Boso was killed at the church door and Queen Brunhild was captured and torn in pieces by wild horses. "These times are like peace, by comparison," said he. And so we came to Wimborne after three days' journey, going roundabout for safety.

Here also after another day or two came King Ethelred, carried in a litter. At Wimborne is a convent of holy nuns, founded long ago by St. Cuthberga, sister of Ine the Lawgiver, ancestor of the royal house of Wessex. In this convent King Ethelred lodged. Each morning and evening he was carried to pray at the altar of the minster church. At first, as his strength returned, he began to try to walk there, supported by two priests, but this caused his wound to open again, and he lost so much blood that he had to return to his bed.

Constantly at the King's side was a man whom I would not have recognized, had it not been for the sign he carried, two arrows bound crosswise on a pole. His hair was now long, without the tonsure, and he had a thick, tangled beard. His torn gown was stiffly blotched with blood, old and new, for, as I learned, it was his custom to soak it in the blood of Christians whom he had seen slain in battle. This, he said, was armor for his body and for his soul. He sat with the King at all meetings of the Council. Wherever he went the King's thanes gave place to him. I did not think he had seen me, for he did not at first seem to recognize me any more than I at first had recognized him. But on the Sunday before Easter there was a solemn Mass in the church, to which the King and all his household went in procession, as he had done at Dorchester the day before Ashdown; only this time the King lay pale, with closed eyes, in his litter. So great was the crowd that half the people had to kneel outside the church, myself among them, and as the procession passed by me I saw Esdras behind the King's litter. He looked at me and knew me. After the service, as the crowd was going away, I found him suddenly at my side. He put his hand on my shoulder and said, "Come with me."

He led me into the church, toward the altar where lay his cross of arrows. He took it and put the shaft between my hands. "Now hold it," he said, "hold it neither tight nor loose. What do you feel?"

I felt only the lightly grasped pole.

"No," said Esdras, "hold it faithfully, listen to it. Do you hear nothing? Do you feel nothing?"

I could feel nothing, only the wood; and I said so. Esdras' eyes seemed to draw away from confidence in me.

"Then you have not the gift," said he. "In my hands it trembles like the spine of a serpent, and in my ears I can hear it hissing like an arrow, or like the wind on the edge of a sharp sword. So, after all, you have not the gift to understand these mysteries. What then became of the mystery you had for the lord Alfred?"

I did not wish to tell him of my failure, and made some reply to evade him. But he knew at once what was in my mind.

"You have not given it to him," he said. His voice was low and hard, he spoke the words as if they were an accusation of blasphemy and betrayal. I could not answer, and he turned away.

I went back to my place in the lord Alfred's house, and again drew out the harness from under my blanket. It neither trembled nor hissed. But the old leather seemed a little softer from the greasing I had given it

before, so I begged some lard from the cooks and rubbed it again, and again I polished the buckles. These I saw had once been ornamented with some sort of raised-up pattern, but it had all been rubbed away till now it was hardly visible. Likewise there were two flat disks on the headstall. It seemed as if there had once been a row of these right across the headstall, but only two remained, crusted with verdigris. Little happened at first when I rubbed them but with my fingers I felt some raised markings, like those upon the buckles. I scraped and polished at the crust of verdigris until I could see on one of them the shape of what appeared to be a fish. Upon the other, after I had worked at it for a long time—very carefully, for it was thin with age—I fancied I saw the shape of a cross, though with something at the base of it which I could not make out.

While I was thus occupied I saw John the Lombard at the door of the house. I called to him, and then wished I had not, since he had been present that night when I had failed to give the harness to Alfred. I did not wish him to see me with it again. However, it was now too late to draw back, so I showed him the marks and asked him if he knew what they meant. He studied them carefully, turning them in the light this way and that.

Then he said, "Yes, it is a fish, and the other is not a cross but an anchor." He asked me about the bridle, but I avoided giving him a full answer. "I ask because it is so old," he said. "I do not know how old the leather might be, but these two amulets are such as

Christians used to wear in the ancient days of the Romans, in the time of the martyrs. The fish was their secret symbol of the Blessed Name of Christ, and the anchor is the Christian symbol of hope."

Stirred by this discovery, I thought that now at last I had a reason for which I could again offer the bridle to Alfred. Now, surely, was the right time.

Alfred went every day to the outlying camps of the shire levies. These were now thinly manned. Hundreds of their soldiers lay dead, or were still dying of wounds they had received in the last two battles. Others were making their way, wounded, to their villages, and with them went many who were sick, for there was now much sickness in the army. And also, since the spring was well advanced and the farms everywhere untended, the fighting men, especially those from the more distant shires which the enemy had not yet entered, wanted to go home to till their land; for, they said, it is plain that the pagans will still be here in the summer, and in the autumn, too, for that matter, after the harvest has been brought in. Then will do as well as now to fight them, they said; but how shall we fight at all if there is a famine next winter because all our fields were left fallow? It is bad enough as it is now, with so much laid waste by the enemy.

This was true. There was much hunger. Both armies were forced to forage and hunt far afield, and many were killed in fierce skirmishes when Christian and pagan hunting parties met by chance at the farm clearings. Yet even in such days as these the hard-pressed men would take heart from the presence and encouragement of their leaders, and when they saw the royal banners of Wessex among their ranks, their resolution would grow warm again. The King had said that when Easter was past, if his wound would still not let him ride, he would go carried in his litter to visit the shiremen's camps. In the meantime the lord Alfred rode out with the banners every day, and in the evening on his return he always went first to the minster church to pray, and then to the convent where the King lay awaiting him, with his counselors at his bedside.

So that evening I put the bridle under my cloak again, and I waited at the church door for the lord Alfred's return. It was late and cold and growing dark, and all the places of Wimborne seemed deserted except where the hearth smoke was rising from a few dark houses here and there among the trees. The nuns came to the church to say their evening Office. A wolf howled in the distant forest. I waited for a long time, and at last, cold and disheartened, I had begun to limp away, when I saw the shapes of horsemen riding slowly in from the direction of Ringwood. As they drew near I saw the lord Alfred riding at the head of them. He was crouched over his horse's withers, his cloak drooping from his bowed shoulders. He halted by the church and with much difficulty began to dismount, but then, seemingly unable to do it alone, waited until one of his thanes came to help him. When he was at last dismounted he walked painfully and slowly toward the church, alone, and I, standing at the door, found it hard to believe he was the same man who had ridden out that morning, so gray-faced and huddled was he now. I drew back without speaking and he passed me without heeding. I wondered what accident could have befallen him, and then wondered why, after a short while, only two or three of his men remained to wait for him at the church door. The others, after some discussion, had gone away, evidently to their camp.

One of the men at the church door I knew. His name was Ulfstan. I asked him what had happened.

"Alas," he answered, "it is the lord Alfred's sickness."

He saw that I had not understood (though again and at once I remembered the words of the monk Oswy) so in a low voice he continued:

"Had you never heard? It is a sickness he has always had. Sometimes for days together he can neither walk nor sit his horse, nor hardly eat a bite, nor I know not what. Then it will pass, and he will be well again for weeks or months together; till suddenly it takes him again just as he stands, no matter where he may be. Sometimes it is not so hard, and then unless you know him well you would not know there was anything wrong with him at all, for he will always bear it out without showing it, so long as he can. But this must be a bad turn he has now, God help him. It came on him this morning as he was riding, and he has been bearing it all day. He refused to turn back. Come to that, I never yet knew him turn back from any course he was on, once he had started on it. If it's right, he says, it's right to the end. If it's wrong, we'll right it as we go.

But it seems there's no righting this sickness of his, go as he may."

He told me there were various accounts of the beginning of Alfred's malady, as for example that he had had some other terrible affliction when he was a child and was said to have lived in fear of blindness or leprosy; that he had visited many holy places to pray that this affliction might be removed, and one day, praying in Cornwall at St. Neot's shrine, he had asked God, not for the removal of his illness, but only that it might be changed to some other, praying only that it should make him neither useless nor disfigured. This, said Ulfstan, was granted him, and he was afflicted thereafter with the ailment he now had. "It is said it first came upon him at his wedding feast," said Ulfstan, "striking him down at the table where he sat. But whether that is true or not I cannot say."

It was now quite dark. In the darkness a woman with a torch came along the path to the church, guiding the lady Elswitha, who passed by us and, making the sign of the cross at the door, entered the dark building. She carried on her arm a great cloak of white fur. "That is for him," said Ulfstan, "for he shivers with cold when he has his fit. But he will not wear it often, not so long as he is able to hide his pain."

After a little while Alfred came out from the church, wrapped in the fur cloak. He said nothing and he walked slowly. The lady Elswitha followed, with her waiting woman carrying the torch a few paces behind him. Ulfstan and the others departed then, each to his own lodging. The torchlight grew faint among the trees behind the convent wall. The wolf howled again in the forest. Within the dark church another noise, not unlike the wolf's voice, rose up to the throne of Heaven from the altar steps. It was the voice of Esdras:

"O God of Jael and Barak, God of Joshua, the heathen are howling in the forest, the Hosts of Satan go with grinning teeth across the fields! Sharpen our swords, O Lord! And the red birds and the birds of blackness shall avenge Thy martyred King on the white tree! Sharpen, O Lord, sharpen!"

I went back to my bed, the bridle still under my cloak.

Alfred remained for two days in pain, unable to rise from his chair. None the less he received messengers from the army. He heard of the burning of Andover, and how Ethelnoth of Somerset with Begni the Hewer, his man, had ridden into the town and guilefully slain ten of the heathen at their plunder, undiscovered in the smoke and confusion of the pillaging.

On the Wednesday of Holy Week Alfred went to Mass in the church, with the fur cloak still wrapped around him. King Ethelred was there, carried in his litter, his wound festering and, it was said, of a very bad smell. None the less the King was strong in heart. He declared at the altar that he would lie in the church from Good Friday till Easter Day, and that he and all his people, his councilors and ealdormen and all his bodyguard, and all men else who would, should keep a fast from Good Friday till Easter, for the forgiveness of sins and the final driving-out of the enemy. And when Easter was past, he said, he would do as he had promised: he would go out to his army and lead it into the field, himself in his litter at their head, and thus they would all fall upon the Danes as they had done at Ashdown, and with the help of the mighty Lord God would trample them in the press of battle till their blood flowed downhill into all the rivers of Wessex. At his words the people in the church cried "Amen!" and King Ethelred lay back again, fierce and sweating, upon his pillow.

So on Good Friday they carried him and laid him in the church. They covered him, as he bade them, with sackcloth, and sprinkled the earth of penitence upon him. They put his weapons at his side, and his golden breastplate and his boar-crested helmet at his feet, and they put the cross of Christ in his hands. Upright before the altar stood the arrow-cross of St. Edmund. Esdras the monk lay prostrate there. The Bishop of Winchester and the Abbess of Wimborne knelt beside the King, and the lord Alfred also. Solemn Mass was chanted and the bell rang all day, while the people knelt fasting, and the sunlight moved around the church hour by hour shining through the little windows high up in the wall. Outside the church the soldiers knelt, each beside his shield and the banner of his thane, while the banners of Wessex, the Dragon and the Cross, stood before them all, hanging motionless in the sunshine. The sun crept across a hot sky all day long. It was not like April, but like a parched midsummer.

And all that night the one bell rang outside the church, and the voices of praying men and women muttered through the long watch. I nodded asleep, but between waking and sleeping all night I heard the tolling bell. It was still tolling when, soon after dawn, horsemen rode into the open place before the church with news for the King. The lord Alfred left the church to hear them. The heathen, they said, had been seen moving in large numbers down the old road out of Reading to Andover, where they seemed to be gathering in force. From there they could strike at either Sarum or Winchester, as they pleased, while the Saxon forces were dispersed between the two. For an hour Alfred sat in thought under a tree outside the church, the fur cloak wrapped around him. Then he sent messengers to Wulfric the Ealdorman at Winchester, bidding him not to give battle, but to be ready to withdraw his men into the forest between Romsey and Ringwood. Alfred did this on his own authority, for the pale King whispering wide-eyed in the church spoke now to no man.

That day was as hot as the one before. In the afternoon thunder was heard in the south. All were now waiting for midnight and the Easter candles. All was now silent except for the far-off thunder and the sound of axes in the woods, lopping branches for the Easter bonfires. There was no sound from those at prayer. The bell was still.

Children had been given a little food, for they were not expected to keep the long fast with their elders. But I would not take it. I was ill at ease. I thought of Esdras and how he had accused me of neglecting my solemn promise to give the harness to Alfred; and yet how all things seemed to hold me back from giving it. I felt I must be to blame and on that solemn Good Friday I had vowed to atone by keeping the full fast. Now I was faint with hunger, and also my leg was painful from wearing the iron harness. All the more, therefore, did I determine to wear it, and all day limped about on it, but as darkness came I could bear it no more and lay down miserably, with aching head and sore body, in the corner of the hut where I slept. Lightning flickered in at the door. The church bell again began to ring, and I heard a sound like laughter. I swayed on the straw where I lay and the darkness swam around me and the bell was ringing fast. Voices of people gathering for the midnight ceremony went past the hut, and the laughing sound kept time with the throb in my leg and the ringing bell. A voice called "Alfred, Alfred," and I tried to answer, but lying in the straw I could not, and the laughter grew louder. The voice called my name again, and this time so urgently that pressing my hands on the ground I thrust myself upward into the air and opened my eyes, and there as the lightning flickered through the door I saw my crutch, laughing. "You cannot," laughed the crutch. I tried to rise, hearing my name called again and again like the ringing of a bell. "You cannot do it," came the other voice, laughing, and as I groped for a hold to raise myself I put my hand on something which twisted and writhed like the life in the spine of a serpent. I lifted it, and heard it hissing like the wind on the edge of a sharp sword. It was the harness. I could feel it trembling. The bell was still ringing and many voices were calling "Alfred!" I hoisted myself upright, standing upon the Dane-leg, and made my way to the door, holding the harness at arm's length in front of me. As I crossed the threshold I heard singing, and saw the flaming lights of torches and candles, many hundreds of them moving among the trees, carried in the Easter procession. At the same time, with a shout from all the people, the bright flames blazed out from the piled-up bonfires in front of the Church.

The harness led me; people made way for me as I went forward holding it out, toward the church. Toward me came the procession, lit by the fires and their own candles. In front walked the lord Alfred. I shouted to him, "Alfred! Lord Alfred! King's brother!" and with the harness I limped toward him. All drew near to me. My head swam. I staggered, swayed, and then fell at full length on the ground. The lord Alfred himself hurried forward, and his face came close as he bent down to raise me. To hold him I stretched out my hands and put the harness around his neck. At the same moment another voice cried out from the dark church.

"Alfred! Lord Alfred!"

It was the voice of Esdras. He came forward into the light of the Easter fires. The flames glittered in his eyes and shone on his wild hair, and only the crackling of the fires could now be heard in the sudden silence. The Bishop of Winchester was with him, and many others. Then the monk Esdras spoke again in a loud voice to Alfred kneeling.

"Alfred, lord Alfred, the King your brother is dead! Pray for his soul!"

"Amen!" the Bishop said and made the sign of the cross. "Lord Alfred, the Kingdom of Wessex is upon your shoulders."

And slowly King Alfred stood up with the harness about his neck.

11

A New Feeling

THE THANES of Wessex gathered for the burial of King Ethelred in Wimborne Minster. He lies there now, awaiting the Second Coming of Christ, beneath the stone floor whereon he died. At that place also, the next day, stood the lord Alfred, to be lawfully acclaimed King of Wessex in his brother's place. This succession was made without dispute, for the son of Ethelred was still a young child and could not lead the West Saxons in the perils that now beset them. Alfred was therefore chosen as being fittest for war, according to the ancient custom of the Saxons, and no man doubted the choice.

But I did not see his crowning. I lay ill, both hot and cold, understanding nothing except that I was cared for, and that I lay under a covering of white fur, which I thought I knew, and which one day I remembered. It was the cloak I had seen upon the lord Alfred on the night of his illness. I saw now that I was in his house, and in the care of his people. As I grew better I learned that the lady Elswitha came every day to see me. John the Lombard also came to my bedside from time to time, and from him I learned the things that had happened while I lay ill. I learned that there had been another battle.

"It was soon, too soon," said John the Lombard. "It was a bare two weeks after the burial of King Ethelred. The heathen beast Halfdan was encamped with all his army at Andover, which is at an equal distance between Winchester and Sarum, and he looked first toward one and then toward the other like a snake darting its head from side to side while yet unsure where to strike. King Alfred sent out his trumpet, his army gathered, and they marched. They stood ready on the downs outside Sarum, and the snake Halfdan darted his head again that way, and crawled with all his body that way, and that way drew up against the shield-wall of our King and showed his fangs. He had been told that King Ethelred lay dead and buried of his wounds. I hear that standing under his flagpole, where his black raven flapped before the battle, he asked what new king the Saxons had dressed for his meat, and his jarls told him it was King Alfred. And Halfdan asked what kind of man was he, and they answered he was a man slighter than his brother Ethelred, and not by nature warlike. And Halfdan asked what heart had he in him, and the jarls answered they would open him up in time and see. That time they have yet to find.

"I was myself in that battle," said John the Lombard, "though I do not know how I came out alive except by the mercy of God, for I am no sort of man to be under a helmet and could hardly have carried my long shield, but that I stood holding it in front of me in the shield-wall, its point in the ground. But the King now needs every man that can carry a stick or a stone, and so I stood there. The King came past along the shield-wall, before the battle, and smiled to see me there. 'Good John,' he said to me, 'we shall value you all the more after today. But do you only fight hard with your shield and keep your sword arm ready for your pen, which I shall need tomorrow.' Truth to tell I did nothing either way that I know of. The battle, when it came, went about me like a tumble in a dream, and when it was over I found I had much blood upon me that cannot have been mine, and both my arms felt much wrenched about and aching.

"We stood all that day behind our shields and the heathen came at us time after time bellowing like bulls, and we time after time beat them back and slew many of their bravest men until it was late in the afternoon. They could not break our shield-row, and we guessed after a little more of this they would draw off and leave us in possession of the field. They made one more attack, bitterly, screaming as they came, with high voices like women, slinging at us with stones and with their throwing-axes and dancing like madmen with knives of iron fire. I was myself tired from all this battle and I confess the sight of them now filled me with fear. But they did not come within striking distance. All of a sudden, as if they themselves had been smitten by a miraculous terror, their wild yelling changed to another note, and they turned and fled, throwing away parts of their clothing that encumbered them. This was a sight we had waited and fought for all day. Our brave men sprang from the shield-wall in pursuit, shouting. I saw the monk Esdras laughing and leaping. He was stark naked except for the shoes on his feet. He carried an ax, and he was shining all over with sweat and blood. The whole Saxon army broke formation and followed the heathen down the hill.

"And then," John the Lombard said, "the heathen suddenly stood and turned upon us and came in amongst us from all sides, and there was a terrible slaughter. It was all part of their cunning. It was planned. Worse than that, it was an old trick. We should have known. We fought hard and we slew very many of them, but we had to re-form into small bands as best we could, and when the night came down we drew off into the darkness and left the field to the heathen."

He told me this as I lay in a corner of King Alfred's hall covered with the white cloak, and as he was speaking the door at the far end of the hall opened and the smoke of the hearth where some of the women were sitting eddied about in the draft, for it was a windy day. And I saw King Alfred himself come in. He was dressed in hunting clothes of fine leather trimmed with fur. He had a company of his thanes with him, and I thought there was about them all some air of ease which did not go with the story of the lost battle which John the Lombard had just been telling me. There had been so many lost battles since Ashdown. I wondered how long it could go on.

They handed King Alfred the mead horn, and as he drank he looked over the rim of it and saw me lying awake there, and John the Lombard standing by me. The King came over and looked down at me.

"Young namesake," he said, "I am glad to see you again with your eyes open. They tell me it will not be long now before you are well, and up on your leg. So now tell me, since God sent you to put a harness upon me, do you remember the one I put on you?"

While I was still calling to mind what he meant he bade one of the women at the hearth, who was plucking a goose, to bring over some feathers from its wing, and these big white quills he let fall on me one by one, drifting down onto the white fur.

"These are your harness," he said, "and while you are getting well, John here shall show you how to cut them into pens; and, when you are up and about, you shall take them to school and practice your letters with them. Do not grumble. Remember your promise to me. I hope we shall make an end of all this fighting before long, and then I shall have as much need of secretaries as I have now of soldiers."

One of those who stood by, Bracwealla his name

was, the King's armor-bearer, made a laugh and said, "Lord King, we have had a day's hunting and it has put us all in good heart; but, for all that, I cannot foresee an end of fighting this year. The summer is just beginning, and the Danes are out to break the back of Wessex. Why should they stop now? They have had the best of it this winter, by and large."

Alfred said, "By and large may not be good enough for them. It is true they have several times driven us from the field; but still we were not defeated. To be defeated means not to return. We have always returned. We are ready now to return again. It is true also that we have lost many heroes and brave kinsmen whom we miss sorely; but that, again, is not to be defeated. To be defeated is to lose our courage."

"Lord King," said Bracwealla, "you know that I am not discouraged. Nor are any of us who are here."

There were many of the King's thanes now in the hall and they had gathered around. They all spoke their assent.

"I know we have courage," said the King, "but we have also something more, which will help us to use our courage to good purpose: we have good hope. We are not ourselves discouraged; but by this time our enemies may be."

The thanes waited for him to continue. He then said:

"Friends, I bid you remember that this enemy, who is so grim and so numerous, is nevertheless not so strong as we. For what is this army but a rabbling collection of godless men, grunting in the midst of the desolation they have made like hogs in their wallow? What comrades have they but other thieves like themselves, each waiting to steal the next man's plunder when maybe he is killed? When they fall in battle they die in a strange land which hated them living, and scorns them dead. And while they yet live, can they ever stay still in one place so long as we of Wessex, even only a few of us, are ready with our spears to face them out? We have here a state and a nation. We are bound together with laws and customs. Our ancestors cleared these forests and tilled this land for us, as our children shall till it and increase it after us. In our Christian churches our ancestors were baptized, and we were baptized, and our children shall be baptized. We who are bound together with these things are strong; and they, who lack them all, are weak in everything but one thing only; that is, their courage. And if we have that thing also, in equal quantity with theirs, then indeed how much stronger must be our reason for hope. Let us also have patience and we may see better times sooner than we think."

The King then turned and went away, and busied himself with other matters. I heard one of the thanes say:

"It is a fine way of talking, but I would not listen to it from anyone else. Yet I think he believes it."

"I think he knows something," said Bracwealla.

Later that day, toward evening, the hall began to fill with men. Outside there was a noise of horses. I saw many of the nobles of Wessex in the hall, Odda, and Sigeric, and Ethelnoth, and presently the Bishop of Winchester. When there was a great number there, and the torches lit and the door closed, the King sat in his chair and they all sat down on the benches in a great square about the hearth. The torchlight and the firelight moved; but the men were still while the King spoke.

"Lords and good friends," he said, "I have sent for you to discuss a certain question which I shall put to you. But first I do not wish you to misunderstand me. I have no doubt of your courage, my lords, and I hope you will have no doubt of mine."

A murmur went up that they had no doubt of it. After a brief pause the King then said, "The question, my lords, is this: Am I to make peace with these heathen?"

There was silence for a moment, then voices from every side broke out, speaking all at once:

"How, lord King? Make peace? They would laugh in our faces. They would tear us apart."

Ethelnoth said, "King Alfred, we have courage, as you have said; but who could have the courage to go to them on such an errand as this?"

The King answered, "I believe we shall not need to go to them. I would not ask it of any of you. Instead, I believe they will come to us."

The thanes were again silent, this time not knowing what he could mean.

"Understand me," King Alfred then went on, "these heathen are all barbarians and men of blood it is true; but that is not why they are here in our land. They

are here because they wish to become men of peace, settled like ourselves in homesteads of their own."

"King, not in their homesteads, but in ours," said one of the thanes, and a murmur of agreement followed him.

"True," said the King, "and for these they fight. But their fighting is only a means to an end, not the end itself. With us it is different. Fighting, of itself alone, will always serve our turn, even if we do not always win. So long as we are always there and always ready to fight, they cannot ever enjoy the fruits they are fighting for. So long as we keep our courage, we shall in the end discourage them. They will think of other places, maybe, where the fruits are easier to get; and they will be ready to go away from here, where their work is so hard and so unrewarding."

"We can fight all the year round if need be," said Ethelnoth, "though if some of us do not get back to our farms this summer we may starve next winter. Better, if we can, to fight for it now in one great battle and make an end of it for good and all."

"Ay!" cried many voices, "make an end of it all!"

"An end, one way or the other," cried one voice above the rest.

"And do you not care which way?" asked Alfred. "Is it all the same to you? I know that feeling well. It is called desperation, and it is next door to despair. Heave up your strength for one great final stroke, it says, and even if you do not win you will die gloriously in the oblivion you have made, pulling down the whole world on top of you, like blind Samson in the temple.

That is a fine dream, thanes, but it is only a dream. It will not happen like that. The world will not disappear because we have died. Something will go on; and what goes on after us, for good or bad, is decided by what we do here and now. I ask you, is there any man among you who can stand up now and say before God and before his kindred that he does not care what happens in the world after he is dead?"

The King waited. All were silent. The King continued:

"I have to preserve this kingdom. By some means, by any means, no matter what it costs in life or work or wealth, this Kingdom of Wessex has to be held together and kept secure. Whatever we now have left, however little, must go first of all to this task. For you see what is happening beyond our borders. All the other kingdoms of this land have fallen. The Danish stream rolls in at every door. Everywhere else the walls are down. The Church of Christ itself is washed away. Nothing stands. Only Wessex stands, a Christian kingdom in the flood. This kingdom I will keep secure by whatever means I can from day to day. Where fighting will do it I will fight. Where bargaining will do it I will bargain." He paused, and then said slowly, "Where gold will do it I will pay. I do not care if this kingdom is kept without glory, so long as it is kept. The glory may come again later."

The square of thanes remained silent but they nodded their heads. The flame of the fire blazed, the wind blew in at the windows, the hangings moved and the shadows nodded on the wall.

"So now I have this to tell you," King Alfred went on. "The Danes are tired of Wessex. Say if you like that Wessex has tired them out. They are ready to talk about going, about marching away, leaving us alone. I know this, because they have sent to me secretly to find out my mind." A hubbub of surprise broke out around the fire, but ceased again as the King held up his hand and continued: "They want to know whether I am ready to met Halfdan, to talk about a price for their going. About payment in gold. A price, to buy them off."

The Ealdorman of Devonshire, Odda, the fierce hater, sprang to his feet and cried, "King, they will deceive us! If they march out of here, where will they go? Back to the last poor man who paid them to get out, to bid him pay again. And then again and then once more. And then in the end they will chop him up and divide his lands, and much good his payments will have done him. And then they will come back here and grin at you again, and hold out their bloody hands for more. And what then?"

"That is the question, Odda," said the King. "What then? Do you think I am a fool? Do you think I trust them any more than you do? But should they come again to Wessex, what will they find? Will they find us stronger or weaker than we are now? Readier, or less ready? If it has been hard for them this time, shall it not be harder next? Thanes, I tell you that if Halfdan is ready to come bargaining with me, I am ready to meet him. But first I will make this bargain with you, that if the Danes come a second time to Wessex they will get no payment, but only a great flea in their ear."

"And what if they come a third time?" asked Odda.

The king laughed.

"The third time, I shall have them all baptized," he said. "We shall have to make Christians of them. It will be the only thing left to do."

This ended the meeting. A few days later King Alfred rode to Shaftesbury and held a council with all the ealdormen and bishops of his kingdom. They debated the matter all day, seated in the church. They considered the strength of their forces, the pressing need for men to go back to their farms for the spring sowing, what money they could raise to pay the Danes, and, if this were done, how then to prepare against the future. No one was glad to have to make such a decision, but all agreed with it. A breathing space must be bought. The next day King Alfred sent back Halfdan's messenger with a careful answer.

I sat outside the King's hall at Wimborne in the sunshine of early summer. Beside me on the bench lay my Dane-leg, unstrapped and idle. Before me stretched on a board was a parchment which I was scraping smooth, as instructed by John the Lombard. Under a great tree in the yard the looms had been set up, and the women were weaving there, while the hall was given over to brooms and buckets and a cloud of dust which the churls were sweeping out. Benches and bright shields were stacked against the wall outside. The tapestries hung like flags on a line between the trees, and butterflies alighted on them. Over the woods the charcoal burner's smoke rose up. Some children were bringing the cows in from the water meadows to the milking. I looked up into the blue sky and became aware of a strange feeling that I could not describe, swelling out from my breast into all parts of my body, as it were into the ends of my fingers and every hair on my head. I felt suddenly happy. I believe it was for the first time in my life.

12

Departures

Messengers went between King Alfred and King Halfdan, and at length a truce was arranged. The two kings then met face to face, at Sarum, to decide the price the Saxons must pay for the going of the Danish host. The conference lasted many days. Both kings had to take counsel often with their own lords and chieftains, and on both sides there were many who were only halfhearted about the peace, so the bargaining was hard. It was hardest of all for King Alfred. Halfdan's price, when it was finally agreed, was very high. I was myself among the King's servants in the camp, attendant on the secretary, John the Lombard. The King's tent was in a meadow by the river. I was there on the evening of the day the gold payment was agreed. It was a bright, still evening, with a swarm of flies dancing in the air over the tent door. Outside, the thanes who had just left the council stood in a silent group. One stroked his beard. Another circled his finger round and round in the palm of his other hand. Another shrugged and walked slowly away to his horse. The King had persuaded them with difficulty. He was sitting alone in the tent when the secretary and I went in, but was so lost in thought he did not at first seem to know we were there. Presently he said very firmly, "It is for the best," and then, beckoning us over to him, turned his mind to other matters.

But it was a heavy price, and the whole summer was spent in gathering it together from the shires. While this was going on, the Danes drew back to their great camp at Reading, and, so that the people of Berkshire should not alone have to feed them while they stayed, levies of grain and cattle were raised all over Wessex. Some new Danish ships' companies that had not heard of the truce came once or twice up the Thames, but Halfdan sent them away. Of the other heathen, it was strange to see that more than a few of them, having now nothing to do, went out into the fields around Reading and worked there side by side with the Saxon farmers. But, later, some of the Danes who had ventured farther out were killed, and there was hard work to hold the truce. Strict laws were made to keep the heathen near their camp, and besides the hostages that had been exchanged, each side now sent some of their leaders or men of rank, by turns, as guests to the other. In this way Jarl Guthorm and his following came to the King's hall at Wimborne.

This Guthorm was of middle height, with coarse red hair which he let grow to his shoulders, and a red beard which he clipped short. He had small eyes and bushy eyebrows. He was very strong in body. It was said that he came from Limfjord in Jutland, the younger son of a large family, who, having no patrimony, had gone viking in a ship's crew. It was also said that being both cunning and brave he soon came to be the foremost in that crew, and then had diced with the shipman for his ship while the man was drunk, and won it from him, and had slain him afterward in the quarrel over it. He had brought his own ship and his own crew when he came to England to further his fortunes in Halfdan's army.

He went hunting with King Alfred in Cranborne Chase and Ringwood Forest. They seemed to have a liking for each other. There was certainly a liking between Guthorm and my friend Guntram the Frank. They rode together very often. Guntram was a skilled falconer, and everything Jarl Guthorm ever knew about hawking he learned in those days from the Frank.

Since the last battle nothing had been seen or heard of Esdras the monk. The cross of arrows which he had put in Wimborne Church was still there by the altar, its shadow on sunny mornings stretching over the grave of King Ethelred. One day in August I went by the church alone. There was nobody in sight. The church door was shut, but through the unshuttered windows there came a strange sound which at first I thought must be of some animal, a sheep or a calf that had been shut in there. I opened the door gently and looked in. There, lying full length on King Ethelred's grave, was the lean figure of Esdras, still wearing the brown, blood-streaked, ragged gown, his hair long and tangled, his feet bare. He lay face downward, clawing with his fingernails at the stones. With his forehead pressed to the ground he rolled his head from side to side. Every now and again he uttered the strange sound I had heard, a high bellowing note from the back of his throat, howling with his mouth closed, and with it his whole body jerked and convulsed. In pity and horror I watched him there for a short while, then, fearing he might turn and see me, I quietly closed the door and hurried away as fast as I could, making no sound with my leg on the soft ground, but hearing still behind me the dreadful sobbing noises of the man in the church.

That evening, when all the King's household were at supper in the hall, with the King back from hunting and Jarl Guthorm at the board with him, and a fine sunset lighting the roofbeams red through the high windows and the open door, through that door I suddenly saw the gaunt figure of Esdras coming in, carrying once again his cross of arrows. The fire-red light of the sunset shone all around him. At first he sat down at the end of the hall among the King's churls. They passed him food, but he did not take it. I watched him. Others, too, turned and saw him sitting there, as the light began to fade. The torches were being lit at the fire when Esdras rose from his seat. He took one of the torches, and with this in one hand and the cross in the other he went and stood before the King and the Jarl. He opened his mouth as if to speak, but he did not speak. Instead there came from his throat a terrible wordless noise, jerked out like the beginnings of words that could not be made. Esdras thrashed out with the cross of arrows toward Jarl Guthorm, who was looking at him unflinchingly with narrow eyes, and then toward the King, whose face was troubled. The King said:

"Speak, Esdras. I will hear you. Speak out."

But Esdras holding the torch, his face bright in the flame, opened his mouth wide and made a noise of hatred that was heard throughout the hall. The King closed his eyes and for a moment turned his head away in horror.

Guthorm said, "He has no tongue. I have heard of this man. It was done to him after the battle."

Esdras spoke with his eyes and made noises in his throat. His eyes glared at King Alfred, meaning to show his hatred of this peace and of the heathen with whom the King had sat down at table. No word could he say, now or ever again. He made a thin wailing noise and suddenly wept. Then he turned and walked slowly bolt upright from the hall, holding the torch and the cross in either hand, and everyone drew back out of his way. He went out at the door and out at the gate and out over the long fields toward the wood on the far side. We saw the torch going distantly among the trees for a time, and then it was gone. So Esdras departed.

Halfdan departed with all his army in September, when the danegeld was fully paid. It was brought in wagons to Reading, guarded with a great force of the Saxons, and so great was the Danish host drawn up to receive it that the wagons came into the field as if between two armies prepared for battle. Chairs for the kings were set upon platforms facing each other, and they sat with their thanes and advisers on either side while the treasure was carefully counted and weighed piece by piece all day long, on a great table between them. The armies, in formation under their banners, sat on the ground. When all was over, the heathen made a sacrifice to their god. They had built a stone altar, and laid on it a gold ring which they believe has power over the sun, and they slaughtered a bull and a stallion and poured the blood of the beasts over the ring. Next morning the Christians held a solemn Mass, and that day the heathen broke camp and began to depart. Among the last of them went Jarl Guthorm. He set his horse toward London, but on the last hilltop he paused and looked back for a long time over the land of Wessex as though he were loath to leave it.

When they had gone at last, we all went into their deserted camp, where there was nothing left in the huts of the brute heathen but old rags and bones and litter, and set fire to it all. The camp was as big as a town and the smoke of it spread densely across the sky following the path of the departed army. Guthorm must have smelled it on the wind, miles away.

All the next winter the heathen army lay at London, gathering strength again as more ships came in from their northern lands, and King Alfred kept good watch on them for fear they should break their bargain and return. But they did not. Black Halfdan had had enough of Wessex. Now he looked again toward Mercia. Burgred, King of Mercia, was a small fat man, and he was in his royal hall at Repton one day in the spring, tasting a pudding, when they brought him the news that the Danish host was marching that way, and had already reached Northampton. Burgred fled. Halfdan seized his houses and lands at Repton and the heathen army settled all about. Burgred sent gifts to them there. This was the beginning of the end of the Kingdom of Mercia.

In Wessex, Guntram was teaching me to ride a horse and manage it with as much skill as if I had both my legs. He had a special stirrup made for me, and a wooden leg which had near the bottom of it a sort of hook, like an eagle's beak, which when hooked into the stirrup, kept me steady and well-balanced in the saddle. The King also had encouraged me in this, and allowed me the use of one of his own horses. Mounted, finding myself the equal of other riders, no longer lurching along as I did on foot, I became eager to be not only as able, but more able than the rest; and indeed with the teaching of Guntram and my own eagerness I did presently become an excellent horseman. Guntram also taught me how to shoot with the bow. He himself was very skillful with this weapon, far more than the Saxons are, who do not much use it. I have seen Guntram kill a rabbit outright at a hundred paces, standing, and at fifty from a running horse. This trick he said he had learned in Pannonia when he was young and had gone there with an embassy from the King of the Franks. The Pannonians live in a country beyond Italy, where there are wide plains and the horses run like the wind, he said, and the riders shoot from the saddle at full gallop and can bring down a sparrow in flight. He used to talk to me a long time about the far places he had seen, and at the end he would fall silent for a while, his eyes dreaming on the distance. "I shall grow fat," he would then say. "I do nothing here, now that the wars are over, but wait for them to start again, which my lord Alfred prays to God daily will not happen. And he is right, he is right. May it not happen. But I shall grow fat. Look, I have already had to make another hole to let out my belt."

That summer the King began to make his capital at Winchester, since this town is in the middle of Wessex, from which all parts between Kent and the River Severn can be reached equally well. He had a great hall built there, and houses for all his following. While the hall was still building and the high rafters stood yet unroofed against the sky, a royal guest came to Winchester, and King Alfred received him under an awning between the new building and the green trees. This was King Burgred of Mercia. He was on his way to the coast to take ship with his family, his cook, and a small company of thanes, for France. He was on his way to Rome. "I am told," said he, "that you have been there yourself, King Alfred."

"I have twice been there," King Alfred replied, "but I was then only a young child and I remember little or nothing of it, except the magnificence of the great church of St. Peter, and the rings upon the fingers of His Holiness the Pope, when he lifted me up. I was hardly four years old the first time I went there. My father Ethelwulf had sent me with his ambassador.

I was the token of his intercession to the holy Saints Peter and Paul, to deliver us from the coming of the Northmen. It seems," he said, smiling, "that I did not do very well on my own, for two years later my father himself had to make the journey, taking me with him. And are you yourself now making a pilgrimage of this kind?"

King Burgred spread his hands and raised his eyebrows.

"You might call it a pilgrimage," he said, "but I plan to stay a long time there. Mercia is in very great need of"—he paused, fumbling for the word—"of my intercession before St. Peter." He sighed. "I doubt, alas, if I shall ever return."

King Alfred said nothing, but looked down and stroked his knee.

King Burgred went on, speaking more quickly. "King of Wessex, there is nothing more I can do. They are everywhere. One can hardly open a door in Mercia but there are new Northmen outside, who were not there yesterday. One owns nothing. One lives nowhere. One's own people till and sow only to serve them, not me. One's own thanes, even. One sends one's orders and hears only laughter when they are given. What can one do?"

King Alfred, with bowed head, said slowly, "Alas, King of Mercia, it is an evil time."

Burgred said, "There is no Mercia. There is no king of it. There is only one Ceolwulf, may his bones be made into jelly, one of my own thanes. The heathen have set him in my place. He bobs and says his thanks to them. That at least I did not do. That at least."

King Alfred, to pass over Burgred's distress, said, "You did the best you could." And Burgred, with a sound of gratitude in his voice, said, "I did. Indeed I did. One could not do more." He seemed to have said it a thousand times.

The noise of hammering from the new hall rafters broke upon the silence that followed. "You at least are hopeful, to be building at this time," Burgred observed presently.

"Like yourself," said King Alfred, "I have to do what I can."

After another pause Burgred said, "You, too, had to pay them the danegeld to buy them off. Just as I did."

King Alfred nodded. "Yes, we had to pay."

King Burgred said, "They will come back. They always come back." There was a hint of malice in his voice.

King Alfred said only, "We will have to do what we can."

That night Guntram the Frank went to King Alfred, who sat reading by candlelight, and asked him:

"How long will it be, do you think, my King, before the wolves have gobbled up everything in Mercia? By which I mean, how long before they turn again this way?"

The King said, "There is Northumbria also. They haven't finished picking that bone yet. Northumbria and Mercia together make a very large meal. Who knows, perhaps I have a long time."

"Could you feel sure of that?" asked Guntram.

"By no means," answered the King, "but I would

act as if I were sure. One should always act as though there were a good future, even if there does not appear to be any future at all."

"King," said Guntram, "if there is so much future as that, there will be time for me to go and return again before I am needed. I ask leave to go from you, King Alfred, for the time being."

"It is no surprise to me, Guntram," said the King. "I have heard it buzzing in your helmet ever since you hung it up."

"You know I would fight for you sooner than for any king or for any other man in the world," said Guntram. "But this is peace, and I am restless. This little fat Burgred is off to Rome. I wish to go with him."

"We shall miss your presence," said the King, "but we would not hinder your spirit. And as I have a letter to be taken to the Holy Father in Rome, you shall take it for me; and maybe in time you will bring me answer from him, if you have not already gone on again to Byzantium."

"To Byzantium!" exclaimed Guntram. "Ah, that city!"

So when King Burgred departed a few days later, with his wagons and litters and pack animals and his well-guarded chests, Guntram, wearing the same coat of mail and the great Frankish helmet in which I had first seen him, departed also. But as I stood watching the last of him, hoping to see him turn and wave, the King sent for me. He said:

"Our world is growing different, Namesake. Now we have to write letters."

13

A View of Doomsday

THE NEXT spring King Alfred began a journey through the whole Kingdom of Wessex from the coast of Kent to the borders of Cornwall. He sat openly in the councils of the shires. He heard lawsuits and gave judgment. He inspected the mintage of coins, and the exactness of weights and measures. In the towns he spoke with the shopman in his stall, and on the hillside to the shepherd with his flock. Along the coast, fishermen in little wild places south of the Forest of Andred, who had never seen a king in their lives before, spoke with King Alfred. At Bosham he put in hand the building of a ship, which was the first King's ship in England, and himself helped to lay the keel of it. Along the north borders of the kingdom, where it was often hard to know where Mercia began and Wessex ended, he talked with the chief men in the towns and larger villages about the need for ditches and ramparts, to guard against sudden attack. This had not formerly been the custom of the Saxons, and the Danes had profited by the lack of it. There were some who talked about digging a great rampart along the whole border, like Offa's Dyke along the borders of Wales, but this the King would not have. "We wish to resist the heathen," he said, "not to wall ourselves off from the Christian people of Mercia."

One day during this journey as we were riding over the Wiltshire plains we saw in the distance that great circle of giant stones called Stonehenge, which most people avoid, since it is commonly believed that they were put there by the Devil, and that he comes back once every year on Midsummer Day to sit in the center, upon a flat stone which lies there ready for him. This stone, they say, is always hot, even in midwinter. The snow will never lie on it, but comes off hissing. They say that the marks of teeth and claws can clearly be seen on the upright stones around it where the smaller devils sit, crowded together like crows, in Satan's communion. We therefore would have kept our distance from this place but the King rode straight toward it. Just outside the ring he dismounted. We did the same, but only reluctantly followed when the King walked under the giant gateways to the inside. As he did so a sudden devilish noise startled us all, and then we laughed when we saw it came from an old sheep which ran out bleating from behind the stones. The churls who were minding the horses made the sign of the cross at it, but it remained a sheep and trotted away by itself to a patch of long grass. The King meanwhile was sitting on the flat stone in the center. He bade the servants bring meat and drink and set it out on the stone, which was warm, certainly, but only because of the sunshine. So sitting around we ate our food while the King talked to us.

"I have brought you here," he said, "because I used to come here as a boy. I loved it because it warmed and stretched the imagination in my mind, and it does so still. I know these stories about the Devil. They are nonsense. Certainly we have forgotten how to make many things such as this, that men used to do in ancient times, and this is our misfortune if not our shame; but it is no reason to bring the Devil into it. I like to come here, because among these stones I know that I am standing where other men like me have stood and thought the same thoughts as I, a thousand years before I was born, and where others like me will stand likewise after I am dead. This place is like Memory itself, turned to stone, and Memory was given to us by God to make us different from the animals. That sheep that was in here remembers nothing, even of her own mother, and her own lambs will soon have forgotten her. But you, sitting here with me, can imagine, as I do, how many ages have gone by since these old gray rocks were first linked in a circle, as far back as the days of the sons of Adam. They were already old in Noah's time. I can imagine how the waters of the Flood came washing around them to the very top, till only the lintel stones showed above the surface in a big

circle with the waves breaking over them. Perhaps some of these stones that you see fallen were thrown over then by the tide, or perhaps by the blundering whales that swam around. I used to think, when I came here as a boy, of Noah's Ark drifting past, or being stranded here on these rocks instead of on Mount Ararat; and afterward, perhaps, when the earth was dry again, Japheth, son of Noah, would drive his flocks in here for shearing. And after his day, many ages later, came Julius Caesar to this place, and sat down here on this stone, where I, Alfred, am now sitting, and thought as I do now of some other man who would come after him and take the same thought from his mind and carry it into the future. Every man is a part of the bridge between the past and the future, and must feel how it stretches out both ways before and behind him. Whatever helps him to feel this more strongly is good. By feeling this, God gives us to know for sure that we are not beasts and do not die as the beasts die. The beasts alone have no history behind them, and no future beyond their own unheeded deaths.

"So I, Alfred, sitting upon this stone, at the center of my Kingdom of Wessex, can see clearly two things that God has given me to do. First, to make sure that we shall preserve the means to remember deeds of our forefathers in the past from which we came; and, second, that in the hard work of our own lifetime we shall have enough success to be an encouragement and an example for the future. That much at least lies in our power. To have more is something only God can give."

He turned then to the Bishop of Winchester, who was

with us that day, and said, "My lord Bishop, you know that there are people who predict the end of this world. When do they say this will be?"

"Lord King," said the Bishop, "we ought to be ready at all times, for we are taught that Doomsday will certainly come when we least expect it. But there are many who believe it will come in the thousandth year after the birth of Our Saviour. Most of that time is now past."

"How much remains?" asked the King; and the Bishop replied:

"One hundred and twenty-five years, my lord."

"So then," said the King, "mankind has only a short time left to make the world a fit place for the Second Coming. We had better be up and about it. We have a long way to go."

So we left the great stones linked in their circle alone on the wide plain, waiting for Doomsday, and the old sheep wandered back again into the middle as we rode out. We went twenty miles or more over the hills, and as we descended in the direction of Somersetshire we had a view of a place called Ethandune, a hillside with a strange white horse cut in it as there was at Ashdown, but hard to see for the weeds that grew over it. Save for ourselves passing, and a hawk hovering, it was a deserted place, and hardly seemed worth a second glance.

14

Guthorm

I WAS told in later years, by those who had known him at this time, how Jarl Guthorm the red-bearded went in to Halfdan in the great hall at Repton, which had once been King Burgred's hall. Halfdan sat far off in the king's chair, with no one near him. He was angry. As Guthorm approached him he frowned and said:

"I will have no more words with you."

Guthorm answered, "King Halfdan, you know that what I have said has been well said, and in loyalty. But since you will not hear me, and since my time of service is now over, I mean to take my men south again."

Halfdan did not answer, and so Jarl Guthorm turned to go. But when he was at the hall door Halfdan called him again. "Sit here by me," he said, when Guthorm had returned. He sent for ale and filled the drinking horn. He held it for Guthorm to drink first. "All day I have heard nothing but anger and dispute," he said when they had drunk. "Three great kingdoms we have conquered here in England. We may now share the lands and live on them, and there is no one to raise a hand against us. Is this not what we came here to do? Why should we not now enjoy it?"

Guthorm opened his mouth to speak, but then thought better of it and remained silent. Halfdan glanced sharply at him.

"Say it, then," he said.

"Since you ask me, I will say it," said Guthorm. "Wessex is not yet conquered."

"When the next man is ready to take it," said Halfdan, "it will fall simply by shaking the tree. Wait for the rot to spread. What has happened here in Mercia will happen there."

Guthorm said, "You would be right, Halfdan, but for one thing. I fear King Alfred."

Halfdan laughed. "So you have said before. Do you think the little man has witchcraft?"

"As to little," said Guthorm, "it was the mouse that gnawed the cable that lost the great ship. As to witchcraft, there may be something in that, too. He has the power to make people trust him. He believes, himself, in this power. He is also very intelligent. These things may not be witchcraft, but they work like magic. I fear that if we give him time to use his powers to the full, he may drive us out of England before we drive him out of Wessex. We must go back against him soon or it may be too late."

"For me it is too late already," said Halfdan. Guthorm did not know then what he meant by this, but he remembered it a year later when it was told him that Halfdan had died of a painful sickness. It was believed that the three sons of Ragnar Lodbrok, Halfdan, Ingvar and Hubba, were able to know beforehand the time of their own deaths. Ingvar had certainly known, and had died on the day he had foretold. It must have been because of this knowledge, as Guthorm thought later, that Halfdan had abandoned the fight for Wessex, and had been content with the easier prizes he had won already. But Halfdan said nothing of this at the time. He said to Guthorm:

"Hubba Ragnarsson, my brother, is in Ireland. He winters at Ath Cleath. They tell me he has a hundred and fifty longships at his bidding. If you are greedy for land in Wessex why do you not join him? His power alone would be enough to overthrow King Alfred, if he chose to raid those coasts. Till now we have had a bargain between us to leave Wessex for my share; but I shall not go south again. My plan is for Northumbria."

Soon after this the Great Army divided, some going to Northumbria with Halfdan, some to settle on lands they had seized in Mercia (or hoping to settle; for though the Mercians had accepted their fate, they often took savage revenges on Danes who went unguarded, or lived away from the great camps); and some, a great number, to continue living as a plundering army, moving camp from time to time like locusts when they had eaten up the land about them.

Jarl Guthorm was now in his thirtieth year, and he knew the time was ripe for him, if he were ever to win great fame. He knew his strength and ambition. Now that Halfdan had gone north and, as Guthorm knew, was not likely to turn again toward Mercia, let alone to Wessex, the Danish army in Mercia was without a king. The chieftains in the council formed alliances among themselves, all for different reasons, having no great cause or single mind. Guthorm knew that if anyone could unite them in a single cause and hold them in it, he might make and rule a kingdom. This he was resolved to do himself.

However, he had to act with caution. Though he was supported by many of the most powerful and warlike jarls, he knew he would not be without rivals, one especially. This was a certain Oskytel who, though he was said to be from Norway, and no Dane, had a power of speech in council which, with his other qualities, had won great esteem with the Danes. Guthorm saw that Oskytel meant to set himself up as leader of those who favored making a settlement in Mercia, as the Danes were now disposed to do increasingly every day. All the more, therefore, did Guthorm turn his thoughts toward Wessex. He spoke on all possible occasions of the still-unconquered wealth of that land. He warned the Danes that the West Saxons were strengthening their country, that they were known to be making earthworks to defend their towns, and that if the Danes delayed too long in marching against them, they might soon find them a foe too strong to deal with. He pointed out also that if the Danes were to allow a strong Christian kingdom to flourish unchallenged along their southern marches, they could never enjoy any of their conquests in peace and security, for if the Christians grew strong enough they must eventually fight to win them back again, and the Christian bondmen of the Danes would undoubtedly rise and cut their masters' throats. Many agreed with Guthorm over this, yet not enough to sway the issue in his favor. Nevertheless, he believed that if by a confederacy of certain chieftains he could assemble a force only large and ready enough for another great raid into Wessex, the doubters and laggards would join them and swell the army. This way lay his chance to become a king of Wessex as well as of the Danes.

He thought at first he would be helped by the incoming ships' crews of hungry land seekers from overseas, now more numerous than ever; but while plunder was still easy to find in Mercia and East Anglia, Jarl Oskytel stood to gain as much support from them, if not more, than he. Remembering, therefore, what Halfdan had said to him, he resolved to go to Hubba Ragnarsson in Ireland—not, as Halfdan had suggested, to offer his service but to seek an alliance.

Thus Guthorm launched his ship again, which he had beached two years since, and sailed from the Essex marches around the Foreland into the Channel. He left behind him his most trusted man, one Torgils Auk, to watch matters in England, and to watch Jarl Oskytel especially.

As Guthorm sailed into the Channel he had the coast of Wessex on his right hand. He steered his ship

close in, so that he could see the shore. He passed along the sea's edge, and viewed the green hollows between the cliffs. On the hilltops he saw watchers, and once he saw smoke, which he took to be a signal. Toward evening, as he drew near the Isle of Wight, two ships came out from the land and made toward him. Guthorm thought at first they were Frankish merchantmen, or perhaps vikings like himself who had been sheltering in the Sound, as they sometimes did, since the Wessex men were no seafarers and so could not easily get at them. But as the ships drew near, the Danes saw not dragonheads at their prows, but Christian crosses, and at their mastheads Wessex banners. Guthorm thought the oarsmen not good; but he saw shields and swords among them. He was not seeking to fight here, especially with two ships to his one; therefore he turned out to sea, and with the help of wind and oar made as much distance as he could between them until darkness fell. This was the first sight the Danes had of King Alfred's war fleet. Guthorm, though he scorned it, considered deeply what it might mean. All the seas and rivers of the world, from the Arctic to Byzantium, were the undisputed highroad of the Norsemen. No king of any nation had ever dared, had not, it seemed, ever thought, to launch ships and challenge them at sea. This was the first time. Guthorm knew that two ships upon the armed sea were nothing; yet for all that he had had to put about, to avoid them.

Later that night when the moon rose and the Saxon ships were no longer in sight he turned again and made back toward the land at Studland Bay. The weather was fitful and he was glad of the shadowing clouds. He ordered his sail to be lowered, to be less easily seen, and bade his men not to speak as they rowed. They then came in stealthily past the sandbanks at the mouth of the great haven or inland sea, sometimes called Wareham Water. They drew into a creek hidden by dunes and scrub at a deserted part of the shore not far from the entrance, and here they lay hidden till morning.

Guthorm knew this place. He had sheltered here before. Six miles inland, over wide water and sandbanks, the little smoke of a village on the far shore could be seen in the light of early morning. The dune where he stood was printed with the feet of sea birds. Gulls floated undisturbed upon the mere. A single fishing boat was far away. He saw no men. During the morning he cast off and ventured farther in. He landed on the peninsula of Arne. From there he could see the town and monastery of Wareham in the distance. He studied the site carefully. Then he ordered a fire to be lit and his men cooked their food at ease. In the late afternoon they again cast off and rowed at leisure toward the sea. The gulls followed them screaming. On the shore, between the Purbeck Hills and the sea mouth, there were now men watching them, some on horseback, who might be soldiers. The Danes raised sail and pulled at the oars toward the sea. At the narrows they were watched as they went through by a crowd of armed men. The big waves swelled under the ship as it entered the sea. The rowers struck with their oars into the deep. The anchorage and the small men on shore were left behind. Guthorm had seen what he had come to see.

Six days later he went ashore at Ath Cleath in Ireland. Drawn up on the strand the hulls of Hubba's ships lay like an endless battlement all along the bay. Hubba's henchmen met him at the landing place.

Hubba, the eldest of the three sons of Ragnar Lodbrok, was the only one to live a long life. He had no foreknowledge of death as Ingvar had, or as Black Halfdan had, who was lying even now upon his bed at York, sick and thin, staring up at the roofbeams of his hall. Hubba was a little, wrinkled, bald man, with many scars. He was one who cared nothing for appearances. His banquet hall at Ath Cleath, where Guthorm was brought to him, was long and low and dark and dirty, and hung all along the walls with the stark shields of his thousand soldiers. He himself sat in his black oak chair like a crow hunched on a fence. His famous yellow beard which he dyed with saffron was cut square at the chest. His clothes were coarse and plain, without adornment. Yet he was rich beyond reckoning from the plunder of half Europe.

Guthorm, knowing what was needed to make an impression in the world, had brought his spokesman with him to announce his name and errand, as only kings and great chieftains are wont to do. Hubba listened without blinking, like a watching snake. Then he made a sign for the mead horn to be brought, which he offered Guthorm to drink though he did not drink himself. Guthorm emptied the horn at one draft. Then Hubba bade Guthorm put away his sword and sit on a bench beside him, and ordered all present to move away from them out of hearing. Then the two men began to talk while the sunbeams from the high crannies moved across the hall and faded into the night.

Guthorm stayed a month with Hubba, and when he left he took success with him. He sailed back up the River Severn, and then took horse with only two of his men, riding ahead of the others to his own camp at Kirtlington near Oxford. Here he learned that Torgils Auk had gone to Bedford, where there was a great meeting of leaders from all the army. Guthorm rode thither at once.

He found Torgils with some difficulty, for the place was crowded. Torgils said:

"You have come in good time, Guthorm. Matters are going your way, though perhaps not to your advantage. There is a new army coming in, more men than anyone expected. You have heard of King Amund, who has been harrying the Franks? The Franks have bought him off, and now he comes here to find another nest egg. The main body of his army has landed near Colchester. They say it is very large, with ships enough for them all and their war gear. There will have to be a new war against Wessex soon, or we shall all be fighting among ourselves, that's my opinion."

Guthorm asked about Oskytel.

"That is why I am here," said Torgils. "Oskytel has come here to meet with Amund. They plan action of some sort. Most of the others are ready to take part in it, whatever it may be. If you have had success in Ireland your vote may decide the issue against Wessex.

If not, your influence will not go far, and we may lose our friends."

"Have no fear of that," said Guthorm.

He went to a meeting of the chieftains and bided his time. He thought Oskytel dealt coolly with him when he came in; but he did not bait at this. At the right time he spoke.

"Chiefs," he said, "you argue how to dispose of these great forces that we have here now standing idle, eager for action, eager for fighting and great gain, eager for hero's honor upon the red-sprinkled field. You look, I am sure, toward Wessex, as well you should. That way certainly lies the greatest gain. A blow struck now and all will fall into our hands. We need not fear that we lack the power to do it. Our own forces alone are strong; but I can add to these a promise powerful enough to make victory certain. I bring greeting to you from Hubba Ragnarsson, whom I have visited in Ireland. He has five thousand men and one hundred and thirty-five dragon-headed ships which he is ready to bring in for the conquest and spoil of Wessex, if we will play our part. Against such an alliance as this not King Alfred nor all his Saxon thanes can hope to stand. I, Guthorm, say it, and I vote here that we march again into Wessex. Let it be in the spring."

This speech had all the effect Guthorm had hoped for. Before that day's meeting was over, all had voted for the new invasion of Wessex, Oskytel being among the first, for he knew which way the wind would blow. Next day he with Guthorm and Amund and only a few of their most trusted followers met again, to begin making a plan. But Guthorm's plan was ready. He advised they should strike into the middle of Wessex, marching straight through as fast as possible to the neighborhood of Wareham Water. Here they would be joined by Hubba, who would bring his forces around from Ireland by sea. Thus they would have the heart of Wessex and all its coastline at their mercy. He suggested they should seize and fortify Wareham, lying as it did at the junction where two rivers ran into the harbor, a place very suitable for a stronghold in the Danish manner. He also suggested they should seize Wimborne with another force, and hold all the country between the two camps. But in this the others opposed him. They considered it perilous to divide the army. Then Guthorm, seeing that he had had his own way on every other point, allowed himself to be overruled on this, though he had misgivings.

So during all that winter the Danish army gathered again into a great host around Cambridge, the same place where it had assembled only a short while ago, as it seemed to Guthorm, for the first invasion of Wessex. But this time the host was greater. The viking swarms from all the coasts and rivers of Europe were here; from the Black Sea and the Mediterranean, from the Douro and the Garonne and the Seine, from the Baltic and the Arctic and the Irish Seas, the raven banners and the red swords came in for the hacking and the carving-up of Alfred's kingdom. "Let him and his Christ God now save each other if they can," said Guthorm, "for Odin's flood comes with the spring."

King Alfred was not without warning. So great an

army could not assemble without his hearing of it, nor without his guessing what its purpose must be. He had in any case expected it. But before he could summon his own forces into the field he needed to know as nearly as possible where the blow would fall, and when. His spies were watching the Danish camps. One of these, named Lecca, a skillful and cunning man who could speak the Danish tongue, had been able to live and go about the enemy camps and send back reports of the preparation for a long time, until early spring when the horses were rounded up and the baggage began to be made ready for the march. He did not know that he had been suspected, nor that Guthorm had given orders to those that knew of it to let him go on as usual; but that he should be given certain false information which, not knowing, he sent back to Alfred. Then, when March came, month of the war god, and when the host stood ready waiting for the trumpet, and the message had been sent to Hubba, and the three kings, Guthorm, Amund and Oskytel, sat armed on horseback before the shrine of Odin, Guthorm's men dragged Lecca half-dead before them. They had taken and tortured him the night before. Guthorm dismounted and cut the man's throat, and poured his blood upon the altar before all the army. So the trumpets were sounded, and they marched.

15

The War in Dorset

MY LORD ALFRED the King was at Winchester when the news came that the heathen were once more in Wessex. I, Alfred the Dane-Leg, was with the Queen and her children at Sherborne. This was the King's favorite manor. Here he kept his books, and here John the Lombard taught the few scholars the King had chosen for his school, two or three of the sons of his thanes who had shown themselves apt, and his own son Edward. When he was at Sherborne, in the intervals of his travels in the kingdom, the King himself came to study with us. As for me, during the past two years I had grown proficient enough to make copies of the letters Grimbald the secretary wrote for the King, before they were sent out. But all that, as I saw now, belonged to a time of peace. It was over.

Two messengers came, almost on each other's heels. The first on a sweating horse brought us the news of the invasion. I felt again the panic of those earlier times, the lurch in the stomach when bad news, long expected but hopefully kept hidden, stands at last in the open, to be dealt with. The messenger was a servant of a thane of Berkshire who had seen the vanguard of the heathen army crossing the Thames. This thane had barely escaped with his family into the woods before the outriders of the coming swarm had seized and burned his house while the whole body of the plundering army trampled on, past the smoke of it, not stopping for anything.

On being told the King was not at Sherborne the messenger was ready to set off again in search of him, but then the second messenger came, from the King himself. His news was that he had already left Winchester, riding westward with a small force, and meant to set up his standard at Shaftesbury until it was known which way the enemy now intended to strike. Their main body was marching from Reading in a southwesterly direction, and it was believed this time they meant to make their main camp at Sarum. The messenger said the King was in good heart, and had sent cheerful greetings to the Queen and her children. They would be safe at Sherborne, he said. As for his army, the shires had been preparing for this blow all winter long, and were already gathering in their levies. Meanwhile he asked for certain men of his household to join him at Shaftesbury, among whom he wished for his secretary Grimbald.

But Grimbald was away at Glastonbury at this time, on an earlier errand for the King; and John the Lombard, who might have filled his place, had lately grown very sick with swelling at his joints, so that he could not sit a horse nor even walk with ease. I myself was therefore the only person on hand who might serve. The King's thane who was in charge of the arrangements sent for me and said, "Young Alfred, is your pen sharp enough for the battlefield?" So I stumped off and saddled a horse and strapped on my saddle-leg, and a few hours later, one of a small company in the ghost-gray dawn, I rode to seek the King's flag at Shaftesbury. I remembered earlier times like this that I had known; and yet how different this was! I was a King's secretary. I rode with soldiers in a proud country. The sun rose over the hill and glittered on our bridles and our helmets, and fired the dust of our galloping roadway.

But the King was not at Shaftesbury. The confusions of the gathering war had begun. The town was in arms. Men from Wiltshire and Dorset were assembling there, but as yet nobody of rank who could direct them. Yet hardly had we arrived when we were greeted by Bracwealla, the King's armor-bearer, who had been sent to find us. He said the enemy had passed through Sarum and seemed to be marching for the coast. The King was in the woods of Cranborne Chase a few miles off. We mounted again and followed the armor-bearer.

In the woods we found Alfgar of Dorset with two hundred armed men from the villages around those parts; but the King was not with them. We were told he was with his bodyguard farther off in the direction of Wimborne. In the late afternoon we found his camp among some sheepcotes in a valley. Outposts kept watch from the surrounding hills. King Alfred was away still, but was thought to be returning soon. His bed had been put down in the shepherd's hut, and some meat was cooking on a fire. Old Britnoth sat by it, prodding the meat occasionally with his sword to see if it was cooked.

"What!" he exclaimed when he saw me. "So here's my young Hop-and-Skip again! What are you doing so far from home? Can you not keep away from the wars?" He told us that the whole heathen army was only five miles away in Wimborne, which they had seized that afternoon.

Late in the evening, while the King was still away, an outpost from the hill behind us came riding down in haste. He said he had seen a great number of men in the distance marching in our direction along the track from Sarum. He did not know who they were. The track was behind us, on the higher ground between our position and Alfgar's camp in the wood. We hastily put out the fire and hid ourselves and our horses among some trees nearby. From where we lay we could see part of the track on the hilltop about half a mile away against the darkening sunset, and along this we presently saw a long tangle of men on horse and foot marching south. As darkness came down we could still hear the noise of them, and presently of their trumpets, but far off, as though they were getting ready to camp for the night. Soon after this the King and his troop appeared among us, and without a word we all mounted and with great caution returned up the valley and crossed the track, now again deserted, which had recently been so crowded with troops. But soon after, when we were back in the woods of Cranborne Chase, another great force of men went by, and in the morning we learned for certain that this had been a part of the enemy host.

The camp stirred early, after the chill night of early spring. The King stood warming himself at a campfire when the first of his scouts came in to report the enemy movements. Soon after, he went into Alfgar's tent and sent for me. When I had explained the reason for my presence he asked me only if I was sure I could do the work he needed, and upon my assurance he bade me sit and take my pen. All that morning, while reports of the gathering of the Christian armies and the movements of the heathen came in from all quarters, I sat writing at the King's dictation. He could not write directly to his ealdormen in distant shires, such as those of Kent and Sussex, since these great men could not read; but he wrote to the abbots of the monasteries there, and to the Archbishop at Canterbury, giving all necessary instructions under his seal, which could be passed on to the ealdormen. He also had me write, as each piece of news came in, a reckoning of all the levies now on the march. He had on the table a map which he had made during the past two years, during his travels in the kingdom, with all the towns and villages marked as nearly as could be to the truth, and on this he placed stones, black ones for the enemy, white chalk for the men of Wessex. We saw here how

the heathen had come right through the midst of Wessex making for the great anchorage at Wareham Water. The King explained the map to Alfgar, and asked what he thought the enemy's position might mean. "Do you not think it strange," he added, "that they should have marched right through Wessex to the sea?"

"It can mean one thing only," said Alfgar at once. "Ships."

"So I think also," said the King, "and very likely a great number. I believe we have to deal with a well-prepared plan based upon war by land and sea together. If this is so," he then went on, "the enemy must and will capture Wareham town. We cannot prevent him. Neither shall we be able to defend any of this land here"—he pointed to the map—"between the haven and the sea. We must be prepared to abandon it. How many people live there?"

"A few fisher people on the coast. Some farmers in the Purbeck Hills. We could get them out if we send at once."

"Do so," said the King. "And there is one other thing to be done quickly. We must not let the enemy keep Wimborne. With whatever forces we have in hand now, however small, while the heathen are still on the move, while they are still scattered and busy around Wareham and before their sea army arrives, we must attack and drive them out of Wimborne. If we succeed in that, we can take heart. If not, it may be a hard year for us all."

But before the day was out, while the Saxons were

mustering for the attack on Wimborne, word came that the place was empty. The pagans had withdrawn from it and marched on down to the coast. At this news King Alfred went down upon his knees, there in the field where he was, and thanked God for it as if for a victory.

"Now," he said, "I know my way. With God's help we can master this war."

None the less it was a sad sight in Wimborne when we entered. That the King's house there should have been looted and burned, that had been expected. But in St. Cuthburga's nunnery many of the holy women had not left before the heathen rode in, and their bodies lay in blood on the chapel floor; and at the minster church where, five years before, I had given the bridle to King Alfred, and where I had seen poor Esdras prostrate before his cross of arrows, and where King Ethelred was buried in his golden armor, the grave had been broken open and the body of the dead King lay stripped and desecrated under the open sky. The church roof was gone, the beams were still smoking, the stones of the walls were hot and black, and the many stinks of war hung in the air like dirt.

The heathen seized Wareham town that day and fortified it in their usual manner, making a great camp between the rivers Trent and Frome. There was a monastery there, but the monks had fled in time. Foraging parties from the enemy camp were soon out among the nearest farmsteads. There was still no sign of any ships in the harbor. One of the Saxon warships that had been sheltering there was no longer seen, and was believed to have got away.

King Alfred moved his camp at once. He planted his banner upon Woodbury Hill, between Bere and Bloxworth, six miles from the Danish base. Here he was joined next day by young Ethelhelm of Wiltshire, whose great strength and renown had won him the rule of his shire in spite of his youth. He brought with him eight hundred men. Ealdorman Wulfric of Hampshire came also, with a thousand men, and Alfgar's troops from Dorset numbered twice that many, since the enemy was in their own shire. The levies of the other shires were said to be already on the road. The King held a council of war and spoke thus:

"Lords of Wessex, here is my plan. We know that the enemy is very strong and will soon be stronger, when his ships come in. We also are not weak; but we have more to do than they. We have our farmlands still to keep. We cannot leave our lands idle, and drain away our men in countless battles as we did last time. Battles bring great glory. Our young men will wish to make heroes of themselves in the bloody field, as they did before. Nevertheless, this time we shall not seek battle. On the contrary, we must avoid it as long as we can. Do not look surprised. This is a war we shall win not by fighting but by waiting.

"Listen: If we act wisely, what the enemy now believes is his greatest strength will in the end turn to his undoing. I mean those ships, which he is now so eagerly awaiting. With these it is true he will be able to harry all the coasts of Wessex. But how much food and forage will he find along those coasts, to feed such a great army as he will have? Our wealth lies inland, not upon the coast. To get it, the heathen will have to leave their ships behind them, and, if we use our forces as we should, that is what they will not dare to do. Let them only march inland, and our soldiers, avoiding open battle, will seize their ships on the coast. Once that fleet is here in the harbor at Wareham the enemy will be tied to it like a hog to a stake. The more ships there are, the more there will be to guard; and the more men, the more there will be to feed. It happens that all around them, where they are now encamped, the land is mostly barren sandy heath. This they may not have known when they chose it. They will have to send out foraging parties very often. These we will meet in our strength and destroy, when they are at the end of their long day's work, laden and on their way back. Whenever the enemy puts out a finger we will chop it off; but whenever he puts out his full body for battle we will avoid him. Thus all the summer long he will eat up all the store he can get, which, if we do our work well, will never be enough; and we, meanwhile, will be filling our barns for the winter."

King Alfred drew a line upon his map from Wimborne in the east to his camp at Bere, and thence south to the coast at Lulworth. Within this limit the heathen might go at will, for a time. Outside it, their parties were to be met by ambush and skirmish wherever they went.

A few days after the Danes had made their camp,

the King rode down to Lulworth, with Alfgar and a strong company of his bodyguard. I went with them. We went roundabout, giving the enemy a wide berth. The purpose was to know the land and find places where troops might lie in ambush. It was a fine spring day with a fresh wind. From the hill above Lulworth the view was clear and sharp all the way to Wareham, seven miles off; but one could see nothing of the enemy at such a distance. In the other direction lay the sea, and, right below us, the cove of Lulworth, hollowed out of the steep cliffs like a nest for the sea to lie in at high tide. Down there we saw a ship at the water's edge, with a crowd of people loading it from the beach. It was the Saxon warship which had escaped from the Danes at Wareham Water, and which since then had been carrying people to safety from the beaches along the Purbeck coast. This is what they were now doing. The people below were mostly women and children from the farmsteads around Lulworth. They seemed to be in no hurry. They were waiting for other families which, loaded with their gear, we could see making their way down the valley to the cove. What was hidden from them, but not from us on the cliffs above, was the view out to sea.

Out to sea coming from the west behind Portland Bill, we could see the sails of three ships; and then as we watched, in the distance beyond these, five, six, seven more. They were far off as yet, but they had a strong wind behind them and were making a good pace.

"The heathen!" shouted Alfgar. "It is the fleet!

Those people down there below, have they time to get away?"

"They have a fast ship," someone said. "With sail and oar in this breeze they could do it if they leave at once."

We started shouting from the cliff and pointing out to sea, but the wind carried our voices away and those below seemed not to make out what we said. Our shouting only increased the delay by confusion. They were still waiting for those on the road.

"Someone go down to them," commanded the King. "Quickly!"

I myself was already mounted and going down the landward slope to the path where the stragglers were. One of the bodyguard came with me. As soon as we reached the lower ground we spurred our horses. We overtook the stragglers and bade them leave their bundles and run for the ship. Three young children we took on our horses and galloped with them to the cove. We shouted to the shipmen to push off. We told them their danger. The stragglers, running up, at last scrambled aboard the ship from the water, waist deep, as the men pushed off and began to haul at the oars. We watched them pull out of the cove, and then their sail filled and they were soon out of sight around the cliff.

As we came up the path again the King's troop was not anywhere to be seen. We went some of the way back up the hill and looked around. We had a view of part of the sea again from here. "The ships!" I shouted to my companion who was below me on the

THE WAR IN DORSET

hill, but he replied by pointing inland. There was the King's troop, some way off, riding away fast. A rearguard had stopped and seemed to be looking back for us.

"Come quickly!" cried my companion and started off again down the hill.

I hesitated; then for a last moment I went farther up, till I could see the whole bay from Portland Bill to St. Aldhelm's Head. All across the horizon the heathen sails were crowding in like a flock of wild geese alighting on a pond. I began to count them, twenty, thirty, forty—there were more than I could count in a hurry. The foremost ships were now near enough for me to see the flash of their oars. Our Saxon ship was already some way off, but I feared it might not make around St. Aldhelm's Head before the others reached it. Then I turned to go.

The King's man down the hill shouted to me once more. At a distance the rearguard party had turned to ride off. Then I saw them stop and swerve aside and I saw their drawn swords flashing in their hands, and around them a crowd of men on foot, closing in. Then at last and too late I realized what had happened. As the King and his company were descending the hill, a Danish war band, on foot, had appeared not far off among the trees. The King, Alfgar and the others had avoided them, expecting us to follow. Our party had the advantage of horseback, and, but for my delaying, might all have got safely through. But now as my companion put spurs to his horse another group of the heathen ran out from the bushes and barred his way.

Before he could turn they were all about him. I saw him pulled down. One of his attackers at once mounted into his saddle and turned toward me. In my haste, as I turned my horse to escape, the stirrup hook of my stump-leg slipped out from the stirrup, and I lost my balance. The horse swerved and threw me. For a moment I lay breathless on the ground; then I tried to rise. But escape was hopeless. The Danish rider was already over me, reining in his mount. Without hope or fear or even a prayer to my Maker, suddenly with nothing in my mind at all, I shut my eyes and waited for the sword's edge and my life's end. But instead there was a long pause and a voice said:

"I know thee, One-Leg!"

I opened my eyes. The man's head and body was a black shadow between me and the sun. Out of the shadow the voice came again:

"I know thee, One-Leg! Do you know me?"

As he spoke he moved away from the sun so that the light shone on his face, and I recognized him. He was older and more finely dressed, yet he was the very same man I had taken prisoner after Ashdown! And how strangely alike our situation! The hillside, the awkwardness of the turning horse, and the accident caused by my leg, even the approaching noise of people coming up to kill the one on the ground.

"But is other way now," said the man, grinning. "Me up, thee down."

Some half-dozen heathen men were now around me. One I saw already had blood on his sword. The man on the horse spoke quickly to them and they held back a moment, talking all at once in their own language, but seeming to respect him.

"Now see, One-Leg, I not forget. You did good thing for me, and I will do same for thee. I owe thee a life, and I will pay. But I not owe thee a horse. I take thy horse. You walk. You go away!"

He spoke to the others and one or two of them, while still the argument went on, came forward and helped me to stand. They gazed with stupid astonishment at my wooden leg and my walk. My horse they took away.

"Go quickly," said the man, "for I not able to help thee more."

But it was already too late. As I turned to go, another small party of Danes came riding toward us. They were led by a big, red-bearded man whom I recognized, from the days when he had been King Alfred's guest, as Jarl Guthorm himself.

"Hola, Torgils! Torgils Auk!" he shouted, and my man answered him. They spoke together in Danish. But before I could get myself out of sight among the trees, Guthorm had seen me and shouted to me to stop. Again the others gathered around me and lugged me back face to face with the red-bearded jarl.

"You, King's boy, I have seen you among his people, I know you," he said to me, and again turning to Torgils he talked briefly in Danish. Then back to me:

"King Alfred, where is he now?"

I said, truthfully in one sense, that I did not know.

"You know, you know!" Guthorm shouted at me.

"You know where the camp is, you know how many soldiers. You tell."

I said again I did not know.

"He is a liar, Torgils," Guthorm shouted again, this time beating his fist on his shield. And to me, bending down and putting his scowling face close to mine, he said, "One-Leg liar lose other leg. Lose tongue. Lose eyes." He then gave orders in his own language to Torgils, and galloped off with his following. The Danes then came around me again, tied me onto my saddle with my hands bound behind me, and we all set off as a troop in the direction of Wareham camp. Torgils led the way, saying nothing more. On the way we passed over the body of my companion lying dead and stripped upon the path.

16

The Dry Summer

I HAD everything to fear. Jarl Guthorm I felt sure would not hesitate to carry out his threats. It was hard to believe I would have enough courage to bear what might be done to me, without revealing the things I knew about King Alfred and his plans. My only comfort, if it could be called comfort, was that since I was sure the heathen would kill me in any case when they had done with me, I had nothing to lose and maybe the whole cause of Christian Wessex to gain by keeping silent. Therefore as I was led along, trussed like a bundle among the other bundles that were now loaded upon my horse, I prayed to God, as King Alfred would have bidden me do, for strength to endure and to keep silent.

The sound of a horn call some way ahead signaled

the gathering of the raiding party for the march back to camp. With all its plunder loaded onto sledges, carts and pole-drags; with cattle, goats and geese, driven, it seemed, all in one unmanageable herd or flock; with some dozen Saxon churls, men and women who had not fled with their masters, roped together and loaded with heavy sacks to carry; and despite all the shouting and kicking of the armed men who surrounded and drove us on, our march was slow and ragged, and we did not reach the camp till nearly evening. By that time most of the great fleet from the sea had entered the harbor, and the foremost ships were already at the river mouth below Wareham. In view of this event the return of Guthorm's foraging party into Wareham camp went without notice. Jarl Guthorm and Torgils rode off at once to the harbor and I saw neither of them again for two days. It may have been this that saved me from the tortures I had feared, for when Guthorm remembered me again, circumstances were different, and he had changed his mind.

Nevertheless my condition was wretched enough. Guthorm's own camp was on the northeast side of the town where there was a loop in the river. The ground there was mostly low and muddy. The Danes had their bivouacs and horse lines on the dry parts of the ground farther off, leaving this exposed part for their serfs, prisoners and cattle. Here I was put in a pen with some sheep, my hands tied behind me, my foot roped to a stake and my wooden leg flung away; and here I lay forgotten for two days and nights. A few lowborn prisoners, like those who had been captured with me, were lodged in a shed some distance away, and every morning they were led off to help dig the great ditch which defended the west side of the town. They came back after dark and lit their fires for the night. When by the end of the first day nobody had brought me either food or drink and I was parched with thirst, I called out to these people for water, but they did not hear; or, if they did, they took no notice.

Since during the day I had lain huddled among the sheep, none of the passers-by had seen me, and I had done nothing to draw attention to myself, fearing Guthorm and the torture. Next morning, however, a man came to drive the sheep out to the marshes and found me lying there. Seeing my one leg he evidently thought me a troll or an evil spirit, for he ran away, but presently he returned with other men. From these at last I got some bread and water, but it was pushed across to me at a spear's length, for they were afraid to come near me. My hands being still tied behind me, I was obliged to lap and eat like a dog with my mouth, lying on my belly, since with only one leg, and that tied to the fence, I could not kneel. The King of Babylon eating grass in the field was at least on his hands and knees, thought I. It was as I lay in this condition that I heard the voice of Torgils Auk above the chatter of the men watching me. After some argument with them he turned and went away, and one of the men came and released my hands so that I could eat in comfort. When I had finished he helped me to stand, and brought me through the camp to Torgils' lodging.

Torgils was sitting on a stool outside the door. He was rubbing his sword blade with earth, to polish it. A few paces off, a swarthy black-haired woman was breaking sticks for the fire. There were always a great many camp women who followed the heathen army. Some had come with their men from overseas, others had joined with them in the campaigns in England. Many had children. I could hear a baby crying in Torgils' hut. The woman rose, and as she passed to enter the hut Torgils told her to bring some ale. When she returned with the cup she offered it first to me, as if I were a guest, and then to Torgils. He bade me sit on the ground.

"You saw that day I would have helped thee go," he said, after a while. "I did what I could. In war one does only what one can. Now you are with us. My lord Guthorm is a great leader, king over many men. I do as he says. Thee also do as he says, and all will be well for thee."

He talked for some time in this manner. He wished me to know that the debt he had owed me—no less than his life, in fact—was now considered as paid, so far as it could be; for now, being Guthorm's right-hand man, he was not going to risk any disfavor by giving protection to me. He repeatedly spoke of Guthorm with the title of king. I understood, however, that though Torgils wished me out of his way, and was making this plain, he was also advising me to make what advantage I could out of some interest it seemed Guthorm had in me. This last thing I could not understand at all.

If Guthorm had not ordered Torgils to find me

and bring me to him, I believe I might have stayed in the sheeppen till I starved. Now, however, he required me to follow him to Guthorm's hall in the town. My stump-leg could not be found, and I had to get myself along through the crowded camp with the aid of a pole. Yellow-haired men digging and hammering, cooking, dicing, painting their shields, combing their beards and hair, mustering for guard duty or disarming after, through all that barbarous hurly-burly I shuffled as best I could without much notice being taken of me.

Guthorm's hall was also his stable, where two fine horses stood. He himself was dressed in a tunic of red silk embroidered with interlaced spirals of blue and gold and yellow. Upon his head, pressed down into his thick red hair, he wore a gold circlet fashioned like a great snake coiled around itself and swallowing a man. He had many brooches, rings and bracelets, and the scabbard of his sword, which lay across his knees, was bound with gold and studded with jewel stones. Some of his bodyguard were with him, but when Torgils entered with me, he sent them farther off, as if to talk in private. Torgils also he waved away.

"Young man," he said to me at once, "when I saw you last you were only a boy, but I remember. I should be a blind man if I could not remember the one-leg. I also remember where, how, everything, all things. I remember that your name is as the King's name. King Alfred keeps you with his family, bearing his own name, even crippled as you are. He makes you learn with his own children how to make and read the marks on parchment. Are you not, then, his own child, you, yourself?"

My astonishment was so great I could not speak. For a moment I wanted to laugh.

"You are King Alfred's son, is it not so?" he said again in a low voice, coming closer.

I was able at last to find my voice, and protested at once that Guthorm was wrong. But he did not believe me.

"I not kill you," said he. "I treat you well. You shall see. But what I may need is that you make the parchment-marks for me to King Alfred, so that he only can read it. I will tell you what to say when the time come. You do not deny you can do this?"

I did not deny this, but once again began vigorously to deny the whole of his first absurd mistake. Guthorm studied my face as I spoke, his own face frowning, unmoving, his eyes half-closed and as sharp as knives.

Before he could speak again we were interrupted by a new event. A tall man, dressed in clothes of a violent richness even more extreme than Guthorm's, with some dozen armed followers, came unannounced into the hall, speaking in great anger as he came. Guthorm rose to face him, his own men gathering around. It seemed as if at any moment the two parties would be at blows. However, after Guthorm's angry reply, the wrath of the two chieftains cooled sufficiently to allow them to carry on a long argument which, being in their own language, I could not understand.

The newcomer was King Oskytel. The quarrel was one of many; for the jealousy between the two had

by this time entered into everything they did or said, either in council or in private. The Great Alliance of the heathens was in fact so weakened by this conflict at its heart that it might not have held together had it not been for the influence of the other kings, Amund and Hubba. This I learned later. Now I watched the quarrel without understanding its significance.

Whatever the matter was, and when their tempers had cooled, it seemed to have been agreed that the affair should be decided in some other place. All prepared to go. On his way out King Oskytel chanced to see me standing near the door. He looked me up and down, and then, laughing, made some mocking remark to Guthorm. Whatever it was, Guthorm replied in anger. I think that Oskytel's sneer may itself have helped to confirm me in Guthorm's protection for the time being. They left the hall then, and I, after a time, was led back to Torgils' camp place.

Now began a summer of formless, changing uneasiness, hard to describe. I lived more or less like a beggar in the camp. Guthorm did not send for me again and I suppose that in the events that followed he had forgotten me. Yet it must have been believed that I was under his protection, for I was not molested, although, as time went by and a growing sense of illluck began to creep into the camp, I knew I was being looked upon more and more as if I were myself a thing of bad omen. Men took their weapons out of my shadow as I passed, and stones were thrown at me more than once.

But that came later. At first for a few days I lived

in the straw behind Torgils' hut, tied up. The black-haired woman brought me food. To begin with she did not speak, but stood a little way off nursing her baby and watching me. But after a day or two she addressed me, speaking in my own language, though with an accent I did not know. She first said:

"Are you a Christian?"

When I replied that I was, she went on:

"I, too, am a Christian. I am a Welshwoman, from the Hwicca country at Worcester. My people were all Christians. I have been baptized. But when the Danes came to our village my family was broken up. I do not know if any are still living. It is two years since I saw my mother and my brothers. I was a Christian then, but now I go with the heathen. When I die, do you think I shall go to Hell?"

I said I did not think she would go to Hell only because she lived among the heathen. Having been baptized I supposed she could remain and behave as a Christian.

She said, "I think Torgils will go to Hell. He told me that he was baptized once himself, but that it was a foolish thing and he became a heathen again. He has spat on the cross. He will go to Hell, surely."

All this she said anxiously. Then she lifted the wrapping which she had around her baby, and showed me its sleeping face. More anxiously still, she said, "My baby has not been baptized."

I did not know how to answer her unspoken question, and after a little while she rose and went away.

I did not see her often after this, for Torgils, willing

to get me out of his way while needing at the same time to have me at hand in case Guthorm should send for me, found employment for me with a shipwright down the river. I was put to calking and tarring. The shipwright made me a pair of rough crutches so that I could get around, and this was the best thing that came of it. I did not stay there long, for the shipmen began to say I would put ill-luck on their ships. Ill-luck was then beginning to be the talk of the camp.

At first all had gone well with the expedition. But foraging parties like the one that had captured me had soon stripped all the nearby country. Ships had put parties ashore along all the nearest part of the coast, and had come back heavy with supplies of food. But this army was numbered in thousands upon thousands. At evening the smoke of their cooking fires spread like a white fog on the summer air. And all around from point to point the smoke of Saxon fires could be seen, from behind that hill or among those trees, guarded by Saxon spears and Saxon watchmen, waiting for the heathen war parties to come out, having to range farther and farther afield in search of food. Fierce fighting took place, yet only by small numbers in sudden places. Never did the Danish parties come back from any foray without blood on their corselets, shields broken, wounded men to carry and dead men left behind. Yet three months had gone by without any great battle being fought in the open field; only the sharp meeting of swords in distant farmsteads, the hundred Danes caught in the burning cornfields, and the storm of arrows that followed the landing parties as with difficulty they pushed off their laden ships from the shore. By midsummer food began to be scarce. It was hot and dry, and the rivers were low. The camp had begun to smell. Hubba Yellow-Beard, the sea king, took all his vikings out of the camp to the Arne peninsula where most of his ships were beached. It began to look as if he might withdraw from the enterprise altogether. If he did this, the other three chieftains would be forced to make peace with King Alfred on the Saxon terms, since without Hubba's ships they could no longer be supplied with food. The quarrelsome rivalry between Guthorm and Oskytel was taken up by their followers. Fighting began to be frequent in the camp and added more fuel to the disagreements between the leaders, when they had to meet to decide the awards of blood-money on behalf of their men killed in duels.

It was now certain that unless the Saxons could be brought to battle, the invaders were faced with disaster. The Danish kings therefore patched up their jealousies, cheered their men with speeches and a great feast to celebrate renewed friendship, and one morning before dawn marched out in three columns toward the Saxon main position on the hill above Bere. Only King Hubba stayed behind with his army at Wareham, guarding his ships.

The three kings, marching rapidly and in silence with their great force, quickly overran the Saxon forward posts, whom they killed. But at Bere Hill they found King Alfred's position had been hurriedly abandoned. His own tent in the valley below had been left with all its furniture and hangings intact, which they looted at once. From the hill above, in the morning light, the Danes saw Saxon detachments at a distance, marching north in a hurry. They sent scouts forward, who later returned with the news that the Saxon army was forming up under King Alfred's flags, the Cross, the Dragon and the White Horse, along the ridge of Charlton Down three miles to the north. It looked as though they meant to give battle. Their army appeared not very large, certainly less numerous than that of the Danes. The three kings decided without hesitation to march forward at once and fight the battle before evening came, though King Amund said if the Saxons withdrew again it might be perilous to be drawn on farther away from their camp. Then, even as he spoke, those looking back toward Wareham saw a great smoke in the air, gray and black in the blue summer afternoon, an enormous fire from the direction where their camp lay. Amund cried, "We have been tricked! This is a decoy! The Saxons are at the camp!" Guthorm declared it was a heath fire and was all for going forward and fighting the battle, now that the Saxons were in view. Oskytel this time agreed with him; but then it was reported that the Saxon army was withdrawing yet again, to some other position farther back. Meanwhile a large body of horsemen had appeared for a short while out of the woods to the eastward. The Danes stood undecided while the smoke over Wareham rose up to the high clouds and spread across the view like a curtain, blotting out the distant shine of the harbor, and the Purbeck Hills beyond.

Then King Amund sounded his horn and bade his jarls lead their men back to the camp as fast as they could go. Guthorm and Oskytel cursed, but did the same.

It turned out to be nothing but a heath fire. The heath and the coppices were as dry as tinder after the long drought. But the Saxons had been prepared to take advantage of this. After the Danes had marched from the camp that morning, small parties of Alfgar's Dorset men on fast horses had ridden close in toward Wareham and fired woods and bushes at Carey and Binnegar and Worgret, and a west wind spread the fires and carried them toward the camp. There were open fields between the heath and the town, so the camp itself was not in fact endangered, but this did nothing to cheer the temper of the army that marched back into the smoke that evening, empty-handed. Next morning the Saxons were seen again in force upon the hill at Bere.

I learned afterward how the Saxon army was disposed. King Alfred at Bere and Woodbury had with him young Ethelhelm of Wiltshire with a thousand men, Sigeric of Berkshire with two thousand, and Ethelnoth of Somerset with one thousand. Ealdorman Wulfric was at Wimborne with fifteen hundred Hampshire men, and there were five hundred each from the farther shires of Kent and Sussex, with their ealdormen. Alfgar with all his Dorset men lay upon Winfrith Heath, blocking the road to Dorchester. Between these three camps lay strong outposts and watching points, keeping the ring around Wareham. There were in all some nine thousand men bearing arms. Each month some of these were sent back and others replaced them from their homes and their farms.

I reckoned that the heathen army must have numbered some twelve thousand men altogether.

17

The Ring-Oath

There was much sickness in the heathen camp that summer. Upwards of three hundred men, women and children died of fever, to say nothing of more than twice that number who were enfeebled by sickness, but recovered. The rivers in the hot weather ran low and stinking in their beds of dried-up mud.

In Torgils' hut the Welshwoman, whose name was Efwy, nursed her baby. It had been crying all night and could not be hushed. She knew it was sick.

"What can I do for him?" she whispered to me. "He has not been baptized. You, who are a Christian, can you pray?"

I told her I thought we could baptize the child ourselves, but she would not believe this. She was sure it could not be effective without a priest. To comfort her and in the hope that good might come of it, I repeated all the prayers I had learned by heart as a boy at Thornham. The woman joined in the few parts she herself remembered, and said all the amens. Then she suddenly bade me cease. Some men were watching us from the hut door. "They will think it is witchcraft," she said.

The men had come from Torgils with orders to take me to King Guthorm's hall. Torgils was with him, and a great number of Guthorm's people. Guthorm, when I entered, asked me at once to say what was needed for writing a letter. I answered, a parchment of sheep or goatskin, a goose quill, and certain nutgalls and other things to make ink. He said, "You must do without nutgalls, whatever they are. You can use blood. This and other things you can get from the slaughterer. But make haste."

It was not easy to find the right things, but by the end of the day I had cut a serviceable pen, after many failures, for I could not get a sharp knife small enough, and having stretched and scrubbed a piece of old dry sheepskin, and with a bladder of fresh pig's blood, I was equipped to write a few sentences. Torgils, seeing I was ready, took me again to Guthorm without delay.

Guthorm was now at the Council of Kings, seated with Hubba, Amund and Oskytel under an awning of red and yellow sails which, held up by painted oars, were spread between the hulls of two ships drawn up on the beach. The prows which curved upward from the ground to the long gilded branching dragon necks of these ships, their dragon teeth gnashing at the sky, framed the four kings on each side. A half circle of chieftains seated in two ranks on ship's benches framed them in front. Overhead, a sky of deep gray made a silence in which voices echoed, and which reflected the weird sound of the wingbeats of seven swans which flew across the scene from west to east, their whiteness dazzling in sudden sunlight against the dark sky, watched and wondered at by those below. It was the seventh day of the month. I describe the scene thus because I have it still in my mind's eye, well remembered. It was here and thus that the heathen had at last come to admit that their enterprise had failed. It was in vain for them to stand up and declare, as they did, that the West Saxons had not dared to challenge their courage or their strength, and that they remained unbeaten. They had not been beaten, it was true; they had simply been made to fail. Their conference now was seeking the way to admit this in fact while keeping it unsaid.

Whether or not he himself still believed that I was King Alfred's son, Guthorm had persuaded himself and others that I had some value as a hostage. Truce carriers were to be sent to King Alfred, to propose a meeting where terms could be arranged for an end of the war. It was hoped, if not expected, that the West Saxons would again be prepared to pay gold to be rid of their invaders. The Danes, while they vaunted their power, were ready to accept a smaller dole on this occasion than on the last, since they had not this time killed so many Saxons or driven them from the field; yet some advantage they did not doubt they could obtain,

even now. To add to this it was thought King Alfred might have personal reasons for buying my own freedom; but I think that in proposing this, Guthorm was as much concerned with puffing up the importance of his hostage and of his own cleverness before the council, as with any good that might come of it in the end.

There were four ambassadors chosen to go to King Alfred, one from each of the four kings. Torgils Auk was to go for Guthorm, and he was to take the letter written by me in Guthorm's name. Since none of the Danes could read what I wrote, I was made first to swear an oath in the most solemn terms, before the four kings were satisfied that I could be trusted. I was told what I had to write, and having written it, I was commanded to read it again to the whole company. I wrote as follows:

> To the lord Alfred, King of Wessex, I Alfred the Scribe, the one-legged, write this. Know, my lord, that the Danes increase their strength daily. Surely it is better to deal with the lion while it is young, than to delay till it fills the house.
>
> As I am the King's son, I swear this is true.

The last sentence I added on my own behalf, knowing that King Alfred would understand its meaning. As for Guthorm, since it was he alone who had conceived this idea that I was of royal blood and had been using it to increase his own value in the market of council, I guessed that whatever he might now think he would not admit his mistake in this assembly.

Neither did he. I was sent back and guarded in his hall, fearing Guthorm's anger when he returned. But nothing happened. Guthorm, as I learned later, had at this time other fish to fry. When he came back he came with Hubba Yellow-Beard, and the two sat drinking and talking for several hours, sitting apart from the rest of the company. When Guthorm at last saw me in passing, he stopped and looked down at me where I sat against the wall. "King's son!" he said, and laughed. He always laughed with his teeth clenched. "Do you think King Alfred will read well the writing?" I did not know, and still do not, what Guthorm thought or meant. There are many things both good and evil that have been said of Guthorm since his day. For my part, I think he was neither good nor more evil than the rest of the heathen. He was brave and venturesome; but I think he was also more stupid than he seemed. He believed himself clever.

Jarl Torgils was away with the embassy to King Alfred. The Welshwoman Efwy came to Guthorm's hall. She carried the baby with her still. It was sleeping. She saw the question in my face.

"He is better," she said. "He will not die now. He began to be better soon after we said the prayers. I have prayed every day since, in the same way, as much as I could remember. The children of the heathen women have died, because they have no prayers as we have."

She spoke again about the need for baptism.

"Do you think there will be peace with the Saxons, when Torgils and the others return?" she asked. "I shall be able to go to a priest then. I will not have my child brought up a heathen."

The embassy returned from King Alfred's camp with little comfort for their pride. The King had received them in a very friendly fashion, seated before his tent with his bishops and ealdormen around him in great state. His tent which the Danes had looted in the raid not long before was now furnished more richly than ever, hung with Byzantine silks and Frankish embroideries. The King's chair was overlaid with embossed gold, and his foot cushion was woven with gold thread. The King listened courteously to what the ambassadors proposed. He replied that he would be glad to meet the Danish kings, and that he would do all in his power to arrange their easy departure from his land. He said, however, that he regretted that no payment of any kind could be raised for them this time in his kingdom. He thought, nevertheless, that since they had come unbidden, it should be no hardship to go unpaid. For his own part he was willing to be generous, and would not demand of them any payment for the time they had stayed on his land or the trouble they had caused his people. He hoped they could quickly arrange a safe departure upon these even terms. Upon receiving this answer, Amund and Oskytel cursed, Hubba said nothing, and Guthorm laughed in his own hall.

A month passed with messengers coming and going between the two armies. The Wessex farmers gathered in their harvest, but the Danes grew more hungry. All cornfields within range of their forage had been burned, all cattle that had not been taken already had been driven out of reach. This was the time when they would have been glad to have held Wimborne, which would have been their gateway to the rich valleys inland. Now Wulfric was there, barring the way. For all their food the whole army now depended upon Hubba and his fleet, which had to raid the farther coasts of Sussex and Devonshire. They knew therefore that they had little choice but to put a good face upon it and settle with King Alfred upon the terms he offered them. They made a show by demanding an exchange of hostages. He agreed, but demanded in return that they should again take the oath that they had taken before upon the gold arm ring sacred to Odin, swearing that they would go from the whole of Wessex peacefully and directly, without making further molestation.

This was agreed at last. The hostages were exchanged, and the place was fixed for taking the oath.

Three of the hostages who came to the Danish camp were lodged in Guthorm's hall. These were Leofa, Celwin and Wulfhere, the son of old Britnoth. All were of noble blood. Leofa I knew well, for he was a young man, not much older than myself, and he had lived at the royal court. His father was King Alfred's horse-thane. We met each other gladly.

He said to me, "You have grown tall and thin in these last months. You look like a man, and I see you have a beard coming. But you have lost your riding-leg. Can you ride without it?" He was a famous rider himself, and loved horses. "I see the Danes have more

THE RING-OATH

horses than we thought," he said, pointing to the fields behind the town where Guthorm's horse lines were. I had myself observed that Guthorm now had a great number of horses, many more than formerly.

"They are not very good horses, however," said Leofa.

On the day of the oath taking, the sky was again dark, curdled with heavy clouds like a gray milk. The summer heat had gone, the dry grass did not stir. As on the previous time, when I had seen the four kings together between the ships at the beach, so now as I watched them ride out along the causeway toward the place where the ceremony was to be, the voices of men talking could be heard clearly from a distance as though earth and sky were one echoing wall, and the feet of the kings' horses and their men on the wooden bridge over the westward ditch sounded like a continuous low thunder. Then there suddenly came a cold wind which hissed along the valley, stirring the grass and the dust and the trees on the heath, and blowing back the cloaks of the soldiers marching with heads bent down against it.

We who were hostages did not see the ceremony at the ford three miles away. The altar of stones was built, the ring placed on it, the blood of the bull poured over; and the four kings each after the other placed his hand upon the ring and solemnly swore to march out of Wessex with all their forces and with all speed, and leave the land in peace. King Alfred and his thanes heard this oath, and the men of the armies on each side heard it, and as it was spoken drops of rain fell, and lightning without thunder flickered from the low edges of the clouds where they met the distant hills, and seven white swans as before flew over from west to east against the dark sky. And as before, it was the seventh day of the month.

That night there was fighting in Wareham between King Amund's men and Guthorm's. It had started during the day among some of those who had remained in the camp during the oath ceremony. One of Guthorm's jarls had been seen in King Amund's horse lines, and it was said he had ridden away with three horses. Some of Amund's men had gone to Guthorm's camp to claim them back, and a fight had started. This was stopped without bloodshed as Guthorm and the others had come back in time to intervene, but later the quarrel was said to have been taken up between Guthorm and Amund in private. Then at nightfall some of Guthorm's men had shouted insults outside Amund's camp. They called out that Amund and Oskytel were women together, that the war had failed because of their cowardice, and that they were now preparing to creep away with their tails between their legs like whipped dogs. At this there began a great fight which spread all through the camp. At the same time the storm which had been waiting in the sky all day long split the clouds open and gushed out with rain and thunder. Many men were killed in the fighting before daybreak, and the rain washed their blood into the ditches.

Next day the preparations for departure were hastened, to break camp before worse befell. When the first parties marched out, Guthorm's men were kept away.

We, as hostages, expected that we would soon be free to go back to our own people. I was talking of this with Leofa and the others under a pent roof, sheltering from the rain, when the woman Efwy came and asked to speak with me alone. I said, could she not speak in front of the others? She hesitated, and then asked that when we went back, would we take her and her baby along with us. She wished to have her baby baptized and to remain among Christian people.

Leofa said sharply, "But how will you live, and who will look after you? Are there no priests left in Mercia to baptize the child when you get back there with your viking jarl? Or will he forbid it?"

She seemed in distress. She said, "We are not going with the others. I am to go in a ship." And she started to weep.

I asked, "Where are the ships going? What do you fear?"

"I do not know," she said. "Do not ask me anything. Only help me to stay here with the child. I am sure Torgils will be killed in any case, and then what will become of me?"

"The fighting is over," I said, "unless the Danes fight again among themselves. How else should Torgils be killed?"

"If he breaks the oath he will die. They will all die," she said. "I dare not stay with the heathen. If you will not help me I will go alone."

She was turning to go, but Leofa caught her by the arm.

"What are you not telling us?" he demanded. "What oath will be broken?"

She shook her arm free and tried to pass him, but Wulfhere stood in her way.

"What oath?" he repeated. "Tell us what you mean."

Weeping, she tried to return the other way. Celwin stopped her.

I said, "Tell us what it is you know, Efwy. If you tell us, we will help you and your child, as well as we can. I promise that."

"But if you do not—" Leofa began, but Wulfhere made a gesture to silence him.

The woman, weeping, said through her hands, "He will kill me, he will kill me."

Wulfhere said, "No one will hurt you. You will be safe with us when the Saxons come. Tell us now."

So at last she began to tell us. She said she knew only a little; but so far as she knew, Guthorm and Hubba were in league together to break the oath they had taken. They planned that as soon as they were rid of the other two kings, whom they despised, and King Alfred being off his guard, satisfied that the invaders were leaving his country, they would break away from Wareham and seize another town in Wessex, in a part still unspoiled, and so continue the war on their own.

Leofa demanded, "Which way did they mean to go? What town?"

She said to westward. There was a place Hubba knew, where he could anchor his fleet in a river.

Guthorm and Torgils and all the men for whom they had horses were to steal out of Wareham by night and ride breakneck over the heath to the west. The rest would follow with Hubba's fleet. Guthorm would seize the town and hold the river for him before he got there. She did not know which town.

"It must be Exeter," Celwin said to us. "That is the only place they could reach riding fast without change of horses, where there is also a river for ships. It must be Exeter."

"They have four hundred horses at least," said Leofa. "Even in small parties they could never get past our watch posts on the heath without being seen. They will be cut off before they ever reach Exeter."

"No," replied Celwin. "The watch posts have been abandoned. If they are sudden, they could be well beyond Dorchester before the alarm is raised. It is bold, but they could do it. When is it to be?"

She said she did not know; but soon. These things she had overheard between Torgils and others, but only in fragments.

We promised that we would keep our word and find protection for her in Wessex as soon as we were free; but meanwhile she must let nobody suspect that we knew what was afoot. She went away frightened. She dreaded that Torgils might find her out; nevertheless we dared not keep her with us then, for we had plans of our own to make.

"The King must be warned quickly," said Wulfhere, "even tonight, if that is possible. Who knows but this night they may ride. They have their horses and their men; there is a moon, there is enough movement in the camp, with all these troops going north, to cover up their treachery. We have no time to lose."

Leofa said, "One of us must ride to the King. Let it be me. If we can steal a horse, in all this commotion I could get clean out of the camp and away without being noticed."

"They keep their saddles well guarded," said Celwin.

"I can ride without one if need be," said Leofa. "But a bridle I must have. That I can hide under my cloak."

It seemed that King Alfred's fortune might once again depend upon the possession of a bridle; but this time, in this venture, it was not I who could help. Wulfhere, Celwin and Leofa set off at once to find out what could be done. I stood with my crutches under the pent roof and watched them go down the path in the direction of the horse lines. Men were going about with their cloaks over their heads because of the drizzle. The three did the same, and so went unnoticed.

18

The Riding

Guthorm's horse lines were well guarded, in case of theft by men from the rival camps. At each place Celwin, Wulfhere and Leofa found watchmen posted, and always within call of armed help. They therefore decided they must watch for a lucky chance. They in fact found a store of horse furniture in a shed not well guarded, and they were able to take a bridle and reins. They might easily have taken the saddle also, but they could not so easily have hidden it, and as it would have betrayed their intentions they left it alone.

Their luck came before long. On the edge of Guthorm's part of the camp, on a path near what had once been the monastery, there was an old stone hut with a roof of turf, which might once have been a monk's cell. It stood apart; and the Danes who had camped in the nearby field, being Amund's men, had left in the morning, so that the area was partly deserted. The three saw a man leading a horse by a halter, who went down the path to this hut, and went in, having first tied the horse to a post a few yards away.

At once, having seen the coast was clear, they followed him down the path. The door of the hut was placed so that their approach could not be seen, and the horse was tied beside the path on their side. Celwin and Wulfhere went quietly past the horse and stood by the hut wall, to intercept the man if he came out, while Leofa began to untie the horse and put on the bridle. Inside the hut they could hear voices of two men. Being hostages, the three were unarmed, but Celwin and Wulfhere had picked up great stones to use if they should have to fight. By ill fortune, as Leofa was fitting the bridle, the horse tossed his head and whinnied, and jingled the bit. The man inside, who must have been near the door, looked out and saw Leofa, and ran out of the hut with a shout.

As he came out Celwin struck him with the stone and he fell. The second man then ran from the hut, having an ax in his hand. Celwin leaped at him also, but he was a big man and threw Celwin off against the wall, and Wulfhere, who was going to the man on the ground, to take his sword, changed his course and grappled with the big man, holding back his ax which he was swinging up. Celwin also rushed at this man, and together they brought him down. Leofa, meanwhile, had secured the bridle, and was upon the horse's back. Celwin called out to him to get away quickly, for they could manage the rest, and Leofa without farewell rode off at once toward the town and the bridge. At the same time the first man rose up from the ground with his head bloody and drew his sword and rushed upon Celwin, who did not see him in time. The sword came down upon Celwin between the neck and the shoulder, and he fell, bleeding. Wulfhere, who had gained possession of the ax, then rose to face the swordman, who leaped back, and they faced each other with ax and sword over the body of Celwin.

The big man was now on his feet again and began shouting loudly for help, while the other, who had been hit with the stone, was still so dazed that he began striking about him at random; and the big man, seeing his condition, took the sword from him and turned upon Wulfhere. Celwin then tried to rise but could not, and Wulfhere, swinging his ax so that the two men stood back, bade him, if he could, crawl to the hut. He did so, crawling in his blood, but stopped at the door, and Wulfhere saw that his life was going. Then Wulfhere in a rage swung his ax and flung it with all his might at the head of the big man and struck him dead where he stood, with that one blow. He ran at once and took both ax and sword from him before the first man could do anything, and turned to kill him also, but by this time other men, roused by the shouts, had come running from a distance with their weapons, and Wulfhere retreated to the hut door, where Celwin lay dead.

Then Wulfhere knew that he, too, was to die, for his enemies stood around him with their weapons upon all sides. The man whose horse had been stolen was shouting out, as more and yet more men came running, telling them what had occurred, but giving himself more credit than he had earned. Now Wulfhere, as it happened, could speak Danish, and understood him. He therefore shouted, standing at the hut door, over the body of his friend:

"Boaster! Booby! You who slew a kneeling man from behind! You who went down at the first blow! You who lost your sword! See, here it is! Which of all these friends of yours will dare come and get it back for you?"

He had thrown aside the ax and picked up his cloak which he held wrapped around his left arm, for a shield. The sword he now brandished above his head, and he shouted again:

"I am Wulfhere the Saxon, Britnoth's son and King Alfred's shield-bearer! Come against me all together, for one by one you dare not!"

Then one of them answered, "Horse thief and son of a horse thief! Your King Alfred is a chicken whose neck we are going to wring. We shall finish you off now, and give him his turn in a day or two. Pity you will not be there to see!"

"Oath breaker!" then cried Wulfhere. "Do you think we don't know your game? You are too late, oath breaker! The trap is sprung, oath breaker! The horse is gone, the King is warned, the game is up!

Come on, oath breaker, and take your death here, before my King gets at you!"

Then they all went at him together with their long spears, but he sprang forward past the points, striking out with his sword all around till at last he grew tired and they were able to close in on him, and he went down shouting his defiance in the midst of them. He gave two more men their deaths before he was done.

But several who were there understood the meaning of his last words and they went at once in haste to King Guthorm's hall. They found Guthorm was not there; he was at the beach with King Hubba, in his tent, and so time was lost; but they took fast horses and at last they found him. They told him how Wulfhere had died and what he had said, and how it was believed a horseman had got away to warn King Alfred. Certainly the horse had been taken, and there was no report that any rider had been stopped on the road. Guthorm sprang up with a great curse and smote the tent pole with his fist so hard that the tent shook the straining pegs out of the ground.

"How long ago?" he demanded. They told him it must be more than an hour, but not two.

Hubba said, "What will you do? If the Saxons get this warning they might very well muster enough men before morning to stop your way. At least they can hinder you, and our plan will not work unless you get a clear start."

Guthorm raged. "What traitor was it who gave this away! When I find him I will pull out his lungs through his ribs!" He pointed to his chief men around him. "Sigurd! Einar! Torgils! Find and fetch me this man, whoever he is!" Then he cooled, and said, "But wait! Not now. There is no time now."

He went to the tent door and looked out at the coming night, which was windy with scatterings of rain. There was a moon rising among the clouds. Then he turned to Hubba and said:

"Old friend and sea king, look at this night. My men are in camp. We have our horses and weapons. We are ready enough, even if not as ready as we would like. Why not tonight? With quick work we could get started by midnight. With any luck the message to Alfred may be delayed. With better luck the messenger may break his neck, though we dare not trust to that. We cannot let this plan fail now, or it fails forever. We must go at once! What do you say?"

Hubba said, "You are right, Guthorm. Even at the worst, it is still worth trying, though indeed I think you will get through. My only fear is for the weather. The wind is strong from the southwest and I think we shall have bad storms. If so, I may have to lie up in harbor here for a while and you will have to hold out in Exeter on your own, till I come. I will join you as soon as I can."

So they parted, and Guthorm rode back in haste to his own lines and sent to rouse all his horsemen, bidding them stand to their weapons.

That evening I still knew nothing of the fight and the death of my friends. I had made my way back to the hut where Torgils had lived, though now he rarely

used it. I expected to find the woman there; and so I did. She was sitting in the shadow at the far end, feeding her baby at her breast. We did not speak at all for some time. Presently she said, "Have you seen Torgils?" and when I said I had not she said, "I dare not see him. He will know I have betrayed him. He will kill me. It was cruel, it was cruel," she went on. "You and your friends forced it from me. I did not mean to tell anything. Where can I hide?"

I told her that she was safe, that she should be quiet, that no one knew the plan had been betrayed. She seemed a little comforted.

It grew dark. She made up the fire to warm the porridge pot, and the inside of the hut became bright with the flamelight. Outside it was dismal, and men kept in their huts. But suddenly a shouting began, first at a distance, then coming nearer. Men put their heads out in the rain to listen. The camp was being roused. A horn sounded. A horseman cantered into our quarter down the main way, stopping from point to point, repeating an order which brought the men out of their huts in a hurry, pulling on their corselets and buckling their belts, not without cursing. Torches, horns and hubbub, weapons and bed bundles brought out, men standing in their companies as if waiting to march off, and then presently, horses. The woman, when at last she spoke, had a thankfulness in her voice. "They are going now at once!" she said. "After all! Whatever I said makes no difference! It is too soon for them to have been betrayed. I have done nothing to be blamed!"

A great, crowded jingling and hoofbeats of many horses snorting and stamping halted outside the hut, and Torgils, dismounted, stood in the doorway.

"My saddlebag and the wolfskin, there, in the corner, get them," he said to the woman. "Quickly! And get thee to the ship camp in the morning, as I told thee." Turning to me he said, "As for thee, do as thou please, get out, away, go!" He paused. The woman was packing the things together. He looked at her, and at me again, and then said, "These friends of thine, the Saxons, where are they?"

I said I did not know. "Ha!" he said. Then all of a sudden his expression changed. He looked again at me, sharp and hard. He looked again toward the woman, and she to him. His eyes began to open wide till the whites showed all around gleaming in the red firelight. His nostrils opened, his mouth opened, his jaw began to move, though without a word. The baby whimpered and she picked it up, still looking at Torgils and he at her. He then found his voice.

"It was thou!" he said, very softly. "It was thou, and the cripple!" He looked from one to the other of us. "Now I know," he said; and to me: "Thy friends the Saxons, I tell thee where they are. They are dead! They are killed!"

He pulled his sword from its sheath, not fast, not slow. The noise of horsemen riding in close companies thundered and jingled past in the roadway outside.

He lifted the sword in a chopping position. He took a step toward the woman, clenching his teeth. She lowered her head with a cry, hugging the child close in her arms. "I punish!" shouted Torgils three times in a hoarse, ferocious voice.

As he raised his sword higher to strike her, trembling in a sort of frenzy, I, standing, braced myself against one of my crutches, and with the other thrust at him to keep him off. He seized the crutch with his left hand and almost unbalanced me. But my thrust had for a moment turned his purpose aside, and before he could recover himself a new interruption held him. Above the noise of hoofbeats as another company galloped past the hut, the voice of Guthorm could be heard shouting as he rode, shouting his orders, shouting to his men by name, shouting for haste. As the voice receded, others took up the cry. One of the troop still waiting outside shouted, "Torgils! Torgils!" The actions of men are often decided by the tricks of a moment. A moment before, and Torgils would have slain the woman, the baby and myself all in one fury. But in the pause, deflected by the urgency from outside, the edge of his frenzy was blunted. He suddenly thrust back upon my crutch, flinging me full length upon the ground with all his force. He snatched up the heavy saddlebag where the woman had dropped it, and struck her with it as he did so. As she crouched down, protecting the baby, he struck her again and again with the saddlebag, and I believe in another moment would have changed it for his sword, but once more the voice from outside shouted, "Torgils!" He stood up and with a kick overturned the trestle and the pot upon the hearth, and without a word rushed out of the hut. A moment later he and his horsemen galloped away, the noise of their going mingling with the other noises of riding, riding, riding from all over the camp, going toward the assembly place.

Guthorm was lucky. Alas, for Leofa and his rash idea to carry the warning on horseback! It had been planned so as to get quickly out of the camp, to outstrip pursuit, and to raise the alarm in the shortest possible time. But the alarm might have been raised as soon, and two friends would still have lived, if we had been content to wait till nightfall, and if Leofa had started, as in fact he finished, on foot.

He had no difficulty getting clear of the camp. He rode around the outskirts of the town and found a great jostle of men pushing across the bridge to form up on the other side for their northward march out of Wessex. He was not challenged. Once across the bridge he turned onto the heath and trotted through the outskirt bivouacs in a westerly direction toward Bere, where the King's camp was, going at an easy pace until there was no one left in sight but a big, thick-bearded Danish soldier wandering about gathering blackberries in his helmet. Leofa suddenly laughed. Peace and the freedom of the wide heath opened his heart. He kicked his heels into the horse's flanks and broke into a gallop. The heath was all hillocks and valleys and sparse trees. The horse was not very lively, but he made it go, exulting in the skill he had. Two miles out of Wareham he topped a ridge and having a sandy slope in front of him down the heather, he urged his horse to a further gallop. He sang in his gaiety. Then suddenly the horse stumbled in the heather and fell forward, and Leofa, riding without stirrup or saddle, was flung headlong, rolling down the slope. He lay there, unconscious, among the rabbit warrens, until the slow rain presently revived him. Getting at last to his feet he found pain in his head, his shoulder, his knee. There was no sign of the horse. Night was falling. He began the long limping walk which now lay ahead of him, keeping toward the west, cursing his folly all the way he went.

Hours later in the dark, after wandering far out of his way, he came to a small camp of West Saxons in Bloxworth Wood. From here, when they learned his errand, several men went with him to help him on his way to the King's camp, still three miles away.

But when he arrived he found the King was no longer there, but at Wimborne, which was twelve miles back the way Leofa had come. But Sigeric the Ealdorman was there, with part of his army; and, he said, Alfgar was at Dorchester, with many horse soldiers. Dorchester was ten miles west, but directly in the line of Guthorm's march. Sigeric did not delay. He sent messengers at once to warn Alfgar to watch the hills south of Dorchester. He himself would keep watch to the north of it. He planned to have his patrols out at first light in the morning. Meanwhile Leofa on a fast horse was riding back to Wimborne to warn the King. It was already past midnight.

But one hour earlier Guthorm, with four hundred fighting men, had ridden out of Wareham camp. They went with the speed of hawks over the westward heath.

At Winfrith they came upon a small party of the West Saxons whom they killed at once, every one, not pausing to rob the bodies. At the same moment that Sigeric's messenger was knocking at Dorchester gate, Guthorm and the four hundred were passing the town five miles to the south. They stopped for nothing till they reached the Rive Axe. Here they forded the river and paused to water their horses before they pressed on. This was just before dawn, when Sigeric's patrols were riding out and Alfgar was setting his guard upon the hills. But villagers met Alfgar as he came down into Upwey on the Roman road and told him what had passed in the night. Then all the morning while he mustered his soldiers, news came in from along the road to the west, where Guthorm had passed; and he had hardly set out on his new march before the messengers came in from Exeter. They told how the Danes had broken into the town before any warning could come, while the market people were setting up their stalls in the early light. So sudden was their entry and so great the surprise that the town had fallen to the enemy without a blow to defend it. When Alfgar reached it that evening, with all the horsemen he could get, he found the defenses secure against him and Jarl Guthorm upon the rampart. The head of an old priest whom the townspeople had much loved, and who had tried to shelter some of them in sanctuary in the church, stood upon a pole over the gate.

19

Farther to Go

The woman sat by the wall weeping and trembling by turns for a long while after Torgils had left. The fire died into its embers little by little. The camp had become silent. Toward dawn I said to the woman:

"We should try to leave the camp. If we go at once while there is so much change and confusion, perhaps no one will stop us. For the moment, we are nobody's concern."

I did not know whether it was true or not, what Torgils had said about the death of my friends. I feared it was true.

The woman tied a large shawl into a sling with which to carry the baby more easily, slung around her shoulder. We set out at daybreak. The rain had stopped, but a gusty dismal wind was blowing from the sea.

The camp was muddy, deserted, and littered with all the refuse of those who had gone. In the streets of the town there was some activity. There was a guard at the gate. They took no notice of me, but stopped the woman. I had reached the bridge, but went back to her. She was almost in tears, trying to persuade the guard to let her through, but they laughed and kept pushing her back. I touched her arm and led the way back into the town. The guard shouted after us, I did not know what, till we were around a corner.

"We must find another way," I said. "If we are to get out, we must do it without attracting attention. You with the child, and I with my crutch, we cannot go fast."

We decided to make for the riverbank on the north side of the camp. The soldiers had had some rafts there at one time. We went along by the old monastery. Just beyond it there was a path leading toward the river, and halfway down the path was a little stone hut with a roof of turf.

The woman said, "You wait here at the corner, out of sight. I can go quicker than you. I will see if there is a way across, and if I signal to you, come down."

She went along the path, but when she had gone as far as the hut she stopped and stood in the path, looking down, and went no farther. After a moment she turned and came back.

"We will not go that way," she said. "It is useless. There is nothing there. Come, follow me."

She led quickly away, and we found another path farther on, which led down to the river. We made our way along the bank, and presently we found a derelict raft half in the water. There were some camp women washing clothes in a near field, but these in a little while marched off. The woman gave me the baby to hold, and got the raft into the river. It floated. It would, with care, carry us. There was no paddle or pole, but the water did not seem deep most of the way. When we were settled, I pushed off with one of my crutches, and was able to touch bottom till we were a fair way out. Then the current carried us downstream past the women on the bank, who watched us go by, but only shouted something and laughed. They went on slobbing at their washing and we floated around a bend of the stream, out of sight. I lay flat and felt down into the water with my crutch, the whole length of my arm, and wherever I could touch bottom I pushed us off farther toward the opposite bank; and so after a little distance we pulled into the reeds and got ashore. As we climbed onto the bank we saw, across the water meadows, the upper part of a great war galley coming around a bend of the river not far downstream. There was nowhere to hide. We therefore walked away at an ordinary pace toward what little shelter there was among the bushes up on the higher ground some way off. All the time as we went we could hear carried on the wind the voices of the rowers talking, and the oars rocking in the oarports as they went upstream to the camp, taking no notice of us. But had we met them on the river it might have been different.

Between the river and the higher ground we found ourselves caught in a wilderness of bogs and marshes. We were an hour or more getting out, and a sorry sight we were on the other side. Our clothes, already wet from the raft, were now heavy with mud. We sat for a while among the bushes to rest, while the woman suckled the child. From where we were, we could see the camp, the town, and beyond the river a part of Wareham Water, crowded with the heathen ships. There was great activity among them, as though they were being got ready to sail; but the weather, I thought, would hardly favor their putting to sea that day.

It was already late in the morning when we set off again inland. It was all heath and furze, still black from the fire of a month ago. We met no one. It was a slow journey, rough and wearying, up and down among gorse and thorn in the sandy hills. Suddenly as she came to the top of a little rise ahead of me, the woman screamed. A man rose up from the heather beside her and took hold of her. Then several others appeared. My heart thumping, I crutched on up the hill the last few paces, and saw on the other side some thirty armed men, their shields painted with the patterns of Wessex; and in Saxon the first man said:

"Who are you? Where do you come from?"

I answered, "We are English, escaped from the Danes. I am King Alfred's own man. I am his secretary."

The thane who led this party sent back his runner, and while we waited they gave us a little food from their wallets, for we had had nothing that day. Very shortly some men came on ponies, and one of them was from the King's household. He recognized me at once. I mounted behind him on his pony's crupper. Another man was told to take the woman and her child on foot,

to a place they named. After this I was among Saxon soldiers everywhere. The heath was full of them. We halted after a certain point among the hills where there was a meeting of many tracks, and here I saw King Alfred's own tent, newly put up, the men still knocking in the pegs. The King himself had not yet come. While I waited, along the skyline went an unending procession of soldiers, toward some gathering place farther west. Thanes and messengers newly arrived waited near me around the tent. Then at last, in the evening, the banners of Wessex appeared over the hilltop, and King Alfred on his white horse rode down into the camp.

He saw me at once and I believe was on the point of riding over to where I stood, but the next moment his attention was taken by the thanes waiting for his commands, and the messengers bringing reports from farther afield, and he turned to them without further notice of me. When all this was over he dismounted, and signed to me to approach. He put his hand on my shoulder.

"Good young namesake," he said, "I feared you were lost to me. I am most glad to see you again, standing so tall. You have grown taller than I in these last months." Then he said, "I understood your letter. But, for a King's son, you are much in need of clean clothing!"

He smiled, and bade me come into his tent and sit down, and had food and ale brought for me, and while I ate and drank he attended to a hundred other matters. Then he questioned me at length about the things that had befallen me in the enemy camp. But all the time, as he was questioning me, I saw that he was shivering a little, and he asked for a second cloak to wrap around him. The old sickness that visited him so often in times of stress was with him still. But he sat through most of that night in his chair with his map on the table in front of him, dozing sometimes, but waking for every messenger, until the one he was waiting for came in the dawn. He was from Alfgar, and his news was that Exeter had fallen.

As was customary at dawn in the field, the chief thanes were gathered outside the King's tent under his banner. Ealdorman Wulfric of Hampshire was there that morning. The King had the chair brought out from his tent, and he sat wrapped in his cloak and bade them all sit on the ground, and there, when he had told them the news of Exeter, he explained what must now be done.

It was clear, he said, that the heathen in Exeter were few, and that they could not hold out for long without help. It was clear also that the great fleet in Wareham would sail at once, if they could, to relieve and support those in Exeter. Yesterday they were busy preparing for sea. Today the strong southwest wind was blowing stronger still, and it was good fortune that they were not likely to put to sea in such weather. Tomorrow, however, or some day soon, they would try to leave. This it must be the first task of the Saxons to prevent. Therefore he meant to seize the ground on both sides of the harbor near the sea, to bring up his own ships, few as they were, and by every possible means try to hold and close the narrow entrance where

West Saxon soldiers

Wareham Water joins the sea. Where possible, single enemy ships seen lying away from the rest were to be captured or sunk by stealth.

Then for an hour the details of the war were planned, and after this the King sent for his Mass priest. The Mass was said, and all who were there received the Sacrament. Then the lords left to rejoin their war bands. I stood once more in the midst of preparation and departure, the call-over of men's names as they mustered in their companies, the shields and hauberks, tents, flags and horses, in the whole wide heath which was as full of men as a town, where tomorrow there would be nothing but empty trampled ground and the embers of a hundred little fires.

The King rose from his chair and threw off his cloak and stretched himself. He rubbed his hands over his face, and called for food and drink. His sickness had passed. He ate and drank standing. He sent for me there, and said:

"You must go at once to Wimborne. My people there will give you clothes, and the smith will fashion you a new leg. Tell him he is to do it without delay. You are to rejoin me as soon as you are ready."

I asked if he wished me to bring the things for writing.

He said, "Do so; but this is not the reason I wish you to be with me." He turned toward me and, looking into my face, put his hands upon my shoulders. "Namesake, you stand now upon the first step of your manhood. Did you ever believe, when you were a child, crippled as you were, that you would ever come so far, or stand so tall? Would you ever have believed, crippled as you were, that you could survive the dangers that have since beset you, and that you would put a harness upon the King and stand under his banner in your own dignity? The worst things did not happen after all. Though harm and hurt come often, the worst things do not happen, so long as there remains anything, be it only one single thing, that we can do or use. This thing we must do as well as we can, and the result of it, however little, will belong to mankind, which lies in the hand of God; and God does not allow mankind to fail. In the end, all obstacles, all handicaps, are overcome. This you have helped me to see. Therefore I have you to ride with me. But this time," he added with a smile, "do not linger behind."

Before I left, the woman Efwy was brought to the camp. The King himself spoke to her, and had his own Mass priest christen the child. It was named Efwin. Myself and one of the King's bodyguard stood as godfathers. Some time afterward I heard that Efwy had been taken into the household of a thane of Hampshire, and was married to his falconer.

Leofa was at Wimborne. He saw us on the road as we came into the town and ran to meet us. He was eager for news of Celwin and Wulfhere. I had to tell him what I had heard.

He said, "I will still hope. It may not be true."

"It is true," said Efwy.

We turned to her.

She said, "It is true. Do not ask me further. They are with God." And she would say no more.

20

The Swans

It was reported to Hubba, the sea king, that the West Saxons had marched an army into the Purbeck Hills, between Wareham and the sea, and had occupied the knoll and fortress at Corfe in the gap between the hills. Based upon this, they commanded all that part of the land as far as Studland Bay. Several Danish ships that were beached near there had narrowly escaped capture. And on the other side of Wareham Water, the night before, a number of Saxons with their swords strapped to their backs had crept out of hiding among the sandhills and swam to a large Danish galley which was anchored off the island in the harbor mouth. They boarded the ship and slew the one man who was on board before he could give a warning. But they found that all the oars of the ship had been taken ashore, and with the strong wind that was then blowing they could not tow it away swimming, as they might have done. So they sank it, and got back safely to the shore, where their army now lay in great strength among the dunes.

Hubba knew that he stood in some danger, and Guthorm also, unless his fleet could sail quickly. His army, even now that Amund and Oskytel with their forces had gone, numbered more than six thousand men, and there was not food enough for them in Wareham, even on careful rations, for more than another ten days. And how long could Guthorm hold out in Exeter, with only his small force against all the levies of Devonshire and Dorset, if the sea army did not come soon? Yet with the weather as it was, the fleet could not leave harbor. The wind hurried the torn clouds across the sky from the southwest, the sea rolled and thrashed upon the shore beyond the harbor, and the harbor itself was heavy with waves.

The sea king with his yellow beard stood upon the little hill at the end of the promontory of Arne, and he looked around him over the wide sweep of water, and he counted his ships riding there, one hundred and fifty, all great ships of thirty-two oars, newly calked and tarred and painted and ready for the sea. None now lay out where the Saxons could take them by surprise. All stores and gear were on board. As soon as the weather eased, it remained only to ship the men and sail.

But the foul weather still held. "King Alfred makes witchcraft," the men said. "We have heard of an old white troll who lives in a cave under the cliff, who

has power over the wind. This troll it is who brews foul weather whenever the Saxon king desires it."

Hubba said, "All this is rubbish! Have we not seen foul weather before? Be patient! If King Alfred has witchcraft, I have as good as he! Do you not remember that I and my brothers were given the power to know the days of our own deaths? I tell you that I do not yet feel my death near me. Till I do feel it, I, and all who are with me, need feel nothing but the expectation of success!"

Next morning the wind was less strong. Above the blowing spume from the sea, blue sky appeared in patches. But from the island at the harbor mouth, where Hubba had now posted a strong force to hold his exit, a boat came back with news of alarm. The Saxons, it was believed, were preparing to block the harbor mouth. They were bringing up great rafts and balks of timber and small boats which, it seemed, they intended to link together with ropes, closing the exit with a barrier from bank to bank.

"It is not possible," said Hubba. "Across the exit is the length of twelve ships. How could they defend such a barrier, even if they could get it into position?"

"Their ships are few, but very large," they replied. "With these the Saxons might defend the center. On each side they hold the banks. They might do us great harm before we could force a passage. Might they not burn or sink many of our ships?"

"Useless!" said Hubba. "They waste their time. But in any case—see the weather!"

He spread his arms to the sky, where the blue was

opening out, and the sea spray which had earlier covered all was drifting away as the wind fell little by little to a soft breeze. The sea beyond the bar could now be heard from the distance, its surges dying down. A ray of sunshine broke through, faded a moment and then broke through again. And from out of the west seven white swans, lit by the sun, flew overhead, their wingbeats harping their strange tune. They circled. They flew around and around the fleet, and then one by one landed on the water, where the sea king stood watching, and in their white and gracious pride they swam upon the softening waves in the direction of the harbor mouth. And this also was the seventh day of the month.

From among all who stood watching this, a murmur went up, and then a shout.

"Why do we wait longer?" cried Hubba. "What better sign do we need? Seven swans upon the seventh day to lead us out, and seven sevens is this day the number of my years! Sound the horn call through the camp! Vikings to the ships! This very day we will sail!"

The sunshine in sharp gold spread out and lit the distant harbor mouth and all the soft sea beyond with welcome.

21

A Gull Crying

THE SUNSHINE spread over the sea and onto the beach at Studland where the timbers of King Alfred's great barrier were being assembled. Five hundred men were working there. The King himself directed them. As soon at it was ready, the barrier was to be towed in sections and kept in position by warships, which, stationed at intervals along it and manned with bowmen, would defend it from attack. Six of King Alfred's twelve ships would be needed for this purpose; the rest would keep station on the seaward side, and come in at any point where danger threatened. These ships were now waiting in Mudeford haven, ten miles away, and would come to Studland as soon as the weather allowed. Such was the plan. Over all this preparation the sunshine now suddenly flooded in from the sea.

Everyone then paused at the work and stared up at patches of blue sky.

"You are looking at our time running out," said the King. "We must launch whatever we have ready, as soon as my ships are here. God send them quickly, and delay the heathen for only one more day."

Later that morning he sent for me.

"I have a task for your sharp eyes, Namesake," he said. "Go with my standard-bearer to the hilltop yonder. If you see my ships coming, raise the standard and hold it steady. But if you see the enemy coming, wave it from side to side."

So I rode up with Escwin the standard-bearer onto the high hill that stands between the bays of Studland and Swanwick. From here in that brightening weather one could see everything clearly all along the coast to the Isle of Wight. Upon the summit we stood in our saddles and looked around. We half expected to find the King's sails already on the sea, out of Mudeford haven; but there was yet no sign of them. Then in the other direction, over Wareham Water, which lay all below us on the inland side, the standard-bearer pointed his finger. "See yonder!" he said.

Far off, from behind the spit of Arne, a long double line of galleys was moving out. Their oars dipped and lifted and flashed in the water. The sea gulls rose up and circled about them in white flocks. At that time even at that distance we counted forty ships, and more were coming. Escwin dismounted and unfurled the standard and stood with his feet planted astride and waved the banner over and across from side to side, from side to side.

It did not seem long before the King and his thane guard reached the hilltop; yet by that time one could count more than a hundred ships. The foremost were already approaching the harbor mouth. They were hoisting sail to catch the light breeze. Upon the hill no one spoke. In the silence we could almost imagine we heard the distant shouts of the rowing masters and the cry of the following gulls as the leading ships passed through the narrows and breasted the open sea. They lifted and fell among waves still heavy from the recent gale, the spray breaking white at their prows.

The King had dismounted, and spreading his cloak on the ground he sat down for a while and covered his face with his hand. When he stood up again he said quietly:

"That, then, is over. Our next task is the march to Exeter, with all the speed we can."

While the barrier was being built the King had stayed in a cottage in the shore village of Swanwick which we could see below us from the hill. To the south, behind the village, the land rises and stretches a headland of gray cliff out into the sea. Out from this cliff, and hidden just below the surface of the sea, lies a dangerous reef of sharp rocks. This place is called Peveril Point. Rising above it, about a mile beyond, from where we stood we could see the cliffs of Durlston headland. Here the coast turns westward out of view, all gaunt rock sheer down into the sea.

On the hillside just above Swanwick there was a

small wooden chapel, a place where a hermit had once lived, where the King had gone each morning and evening to say his prayers. He now ordered his thanes to ride at once to the leaders of the army, bidding them meet him at this chapel as soon as might be, for a council of war. He had to know which troops would be ready to march with him that night.

Then the King, with only myself and Escwin and Bracwealla the shield-bearer, and two others, rode down the hill toward Swanwick. As we went we could see, two miles from the land, the whole Danish fleet, its sails spread and full in the favoring wind, dipping and trimming on its outward way in all the splendor of its pride. Like a flock of dragon-headed swans, their gilded necks flashing to the sun, the leading ships, far out, went beyond Durlston Head, turning to the southwest.

But as we mounted the hill toward the chapel a cloud passed over the sun. The air became cold suddenly. The sea went gray. As the King dismounted at the chapel door the wind dropped. There came a hush. We heard the waves on the beach, and the gulls crying below the cliff. The great fleet stood still upon the sea, far and near. The sails began to come down. In the nearest ships we could see the oars being thrust out. They dipped and pulled, and the ships began to move again. The sky darkened.

A shadow passed over the sea as though the monster Leviathan himself, swimming up from the deep, had suddenly broken the surface with his dark body, and at the same moment, like the galloping approach of a great howling trumpet, as if the walls of all the winds had been burst open and the gates of all the storms had been torn from their towers and flung down headlong into the sea, came a vast gale roaring back from the southwest toward the land. Along with it, rolling forward in tumult from the black horizon, came, rank upon rank, an overwhelming host of tumbling waves, huge as hillsides, their crests hidden in clouds of foam, surging down upon the heathen ships which lay now helpless and hopeless in their tremendous path.

The ships nearest that part of the cliff where we stood, having the wind directly in their teeth and not yet having rounded Durlston Head, at once began to go about, hoping to run back before the storm into the shelter of the harbor. Three of them did so; but the one nearest the shore, caught broadside in a great wave as it turned, lay half-swamped, her crew baling for their lives, a few only left at the oars to keep the ship stern to tide as best they could. Thus they were swept along toward the reef at Peveril Point. Too late they saw their peril. The white surge over the rocks folded them in. The following wave burst over them. Pieces of broken wood tangled in foam were all that remained. Following quickly behind them another ship, seeing what had happened, was straining with all its oars to pull out beyond the reef before it struck. But it was too late. The ship was caught, swamped, lifted and burst open, its crew all swept away at once, not one man ever to be seen again.

A pelting rain now came down upon us, covering

the sea with its veils and intermittently hiding all the hundred ships that lay out there in the dark gray water, between the tumbling crested waves. Wrapping his cloak tightly around him the King struggled against the wind, around the side of the hill toward the sea. We followed him, climbing upward toward the crest of Durlston Head. As we approached the top we heard the waves thundering below us, the wind around us, and above us the screaming of a gull.

From the headland, crouching close to the ground to save ourselves from being thrown over by the gale, we could see at last among the veils of rain the whole terrible desolation of the heathen fleet. Here and there, far out, a few ships only, widely scattered, were managing somehow to ride the storm and keep their distance from the wall of cliffs toward which all the rest, in spite of every effort, all exertion, all skill of seamanship, were being thrust and driven by the storm. Directly below us a crowd of seven ships all at once, some rolling with their keels uppermost, others washing back and forth quite empty, others with men still clinging to the thwarts, were being dashed together upon the rocks. They were hauled away again by the sucking waves, and again dashed forward, time after time, breaking and breaking into pieces. A little farther off other ships were being blown toward the same fate. We saw hulls awash, themselves hardly visible above water, the outline seen only by men still clinging along the gunwales. Some, those who had the strength, were climbing aboard, from the sea without to the sea within, where other comrades lay drowned under

their feet. Those still holding to the outside were crushed by the neighboring wrecks which the sea rolled down upon them. We saw one great dragon head, its prow and neck rearing like a sea monster, its body all submerged, riding upon a green wave toward the rocks. Half-drowned men were clinging to the neck all the way up. One of these had at last succeeded in scrambling up onto the head itself when, perhaps by the overbalance of this final weight, the whole monster rolled sideways and disappeared into the sea. All along that dreadful coast, among the white bursting waves under the cliffs and upon the hidden fangs of Peveril Point, the heathen fleet was being torn to pieces. And over it all we heard the loud laughing scream of the gull.

"The oath breakers!" shouted Escwin to the King. "God has broken them!"

Behind and above us the cry of the gull sounded again, nearer and louder, a terrible note. It was like no gull of the earthly sky, but a demon in the red sky of Hell, full of shrill vengeance and laughter, like knives and trumpets. With sudden fear I turned my head and looked behind me. Then indeed I saw it was no gull. On the crest of the hill not far away, stark and gaunt against the storm, his arms raised above his head, thin as a skeleton, white-headed, white-bearded, his white rags flapping around him in the wind, the terrible figure of a man stood screaming and yelling, a wordless noise like some awful human bird. He was coming down the slope toward us. He came to the very edge of the cliff. Then he turned and faced the

King, and thrust out one bony arm, pointing with this toward the sea where the great wrecked fleet was being swallowed up. The other arm he held out toward the King, and there in his hand we saw a thing like a cross, two sticks tied together, two old arrows, their fledging nearly gone, their barbed heads broken and red with rust.

The King took his own cloak and wrapped it around the poor, mad body of Esdras, who did not resist. We led him away down the hill to the chapel, out of the storm. He sat there crowing and laughing his horrible tongueless noise, still holding with both his hands the cross of arrows he had taken from the body of the martyred King Edmund, while Alfred fed him and gave him drink. And presently, outside, the leaders of the shire levies began to arrive for the council of war.

The storm blew itself out in the evening. But that day, among high trampling waves, amid seaweed, stones and fishes; against towers of rock and in cataracts of drowned shingle; under the gull's yell and the hard, blind wind; in the grinding surf-race and mill-brawl of the tide, there were broken and torn and flung into bobbing pieces one hundred and twenty heathen ships and five thousand heathen men.

Laus Deo qui in coelis regnit.

22

Parting Words

Hubba the sea king was right in his knowledge he would not die. His ship was one of the few which survived the storm. Sailing ahead of the fleet he was already well beyond St. Aldhelm's Head when the gale broke, and though he was driven like the others toward the bitter shore, he was able by skill and good fortune to make his way to shelter in Lulworth Cove. Two days later he reached Exeter and met Guthorm again. A few others of his ships came in later to repair their damage. They did not stay longer than they needed. The West Saxons lay about Exeter with an army outnumbering the Danes by four to one, and King Alfred could call upon as many more again, at need. Hubba sailed back to Ireland with what remained of his fleet, and advising Guthorm to make peace with King Alfred, if he could.

Guthorm sat on grimly with his four hundred in Exeter all that winter. They ate their horses. But by the end of February they knew they must make what terms they could while they still had the strength to fight, since fighting might in the end be all that was left to them. Odda, the Ealdorman of Devonshire, whose lands they had invaded, would have shown no mercy to any man of them. He would have had their skins nailed to the church doors. But King Alfred would have no such thing. He received Guthorm's messengers with courtesy. He made no demands except that the Danes should go at once, leaving only their shields behind them as trophies to satisfy the Saxons; even their swords they might take with them, since, he said, it was useless to deprive them today of what they would be certain to make again tomorrow. He did not wish to dishonor them, but only to be rid of them.

March that year was a warm month and the buds were early. Guthorm's army went this time mostly on foot, northeastward through Somerset toward Mercia. King Alfred himself rode with Guthorm part of the way, bringing his own bodyguard, well armed. He did this because he secretly feared many of the West Saxons would have fallen upon the Danes and massacred them in the Somerset marches or in Selwood Forest if he had not been there. Guthorm said to him as they rode:

"King Alfred, men have said that you are wise. What will they say now? You know us. We are vikings, death givers, sea thieves, land thieves. We give no pledge that can be trusted. We live to fight and are not afraid to die. Yet you let us go out of your land like this, without a battle. You might have slain us all. Men will tell you we would have been better dead."

The King answered, "No good can come solely by hastening the deaths of other men. Though the brave man will face his enemy and follow his lord in battle to the death, there is no value in fighting without necessity, and no virtue in either killing or dying for its own sake."

"We of the north think differently," said Guthorm. "We think to die in battle is the noblest end of a man. The blood-red battlefield is the pathway to Valhalla, where the warrior who has died fighting lives again, crowned forever in the glory of his battle deeds. That is why our young men seek the battle so eagerly, why they rejoice to kill and be killed. This is what has made us strong. This in the end will make us masters of the world."

"And what will you do in the world when you have mastered it?" asked the King. "Will you not then try to live, and keep it in peace while you can? Or is Valhalla all you fight for?"

Guthorm did not directly answer this. His tone, when he spoke again, was bitter. He said, "You have cheated us, King Alfred, in spite of all your fine words. Had you come against us in open battle last summer when we were strong, we should have beaten you. Yet you lay like a fox in a bush and dared not show yourself. We were beaten in the end, but not by you. We were destroyed by ill luck, by misfortune, by a storm at sea, not by any deeds of the Saxons. You have cheated us of our glory, but cannot claim it for yourselves. You were only lucky."

"Luck is like seed," replied King Alfred. "It thrives best where the ground has been prepared to receive it. If we had not been lucky this time, we were prepared to go on working till the next. That is all I can say in answer to your charge. Meanwhile I am grateful for God's mercy."

"God's mercy!" exclaimed Guthorm. "King Alfred, I do not understand this kind of religion."

"Guthorm, if ever you come into my land again I will myself instruct you in it," answered the King.

But as to how Guthorm came to Wessex again, how he shook the kingdom, how the great battle was fought at Ethandune, and how in the end King Alfred instructed Guthorm, that is another story.

Here, then, I must pause. The hand is old and cramped with so much writing, the heart saddened, even in this peaceful evening, with all the memory of so long ago, and so long a road between. O, Alfred, my King and Namesake, this peace is the peace you made for us with hardship, and this fine evening, which brings on the night for all men, brings no darkness to your great fame. If time is yet given to me I will write more. But here I pause.

I have been again today to the Abbey church, to the tomb of the Holy Martyr Edmund. He, too, should not be forgotten. He, too, helped in his own way to make this peaceful evening. For, as King Alfred once said, the worst things do not happen. The lives of martyrs indeed are not lost, but are added to the lifetime of mankind.

And there at last, upon the tomb of King Edmund, now rests the cross of arrows that Esdras once took from his body. It was left to me, Alfred the Dane-Leg, in my old age, to give them back to him.

ABOUT THE AUTHOR

This is the fourth book written by C. Walter Hodges, who once said that he wished to "continue to the end of his life in the peaceful occupation of an illustrator." He has revoked that decision many times since. Born in England where he still lives, he was introduced to this country as a writer as well as illustrator with the "noble and moving book" *(Horn Book) Columbus Sails,* the story of a tenacious admiral and a frightened crew.

During World War II he wrote and illustrated *Sky High, The Story of a House that Flew.* It was written primarily for a young son, but was as eagerly devoured by Captain Hodges' staff officers. *Shakespeare and the Players* was his third book, acclaimed for the same qualities of vividness and distinction that make *Columbus Sails* a continued favorite.

With *The Namesake,* Mr. Hodges proves once again that he is both a master storyteller and an artist of rare distinction.